AAK-6420

The Bible
in the
Early Middle Ages

D0149112

Scholars Press
Reprints and Translations Series

Published through the cooperation and support of the American Academy of Religion, the Society of Biblical Literature, the American Society of Papyrologists, the American Philological Association, and Brown Judaic Studies.

Editorial Board

Paul Achtemeier
Union Theological Seminary
Richmond, Virginia

Elizabeth Clark
Duke University Divinity School

John Dillenberger
Berkeley, California

Ernest Frerichs
Program in Judaic Studies
Brown University

Joseph Kitagawa
The Divinity School
University of Chicago

Ludwig Koenen
Department of Classical Studies
University of Michigan

Roland E. Murphy
Duke University Divinity School

Jacob Neusner
Program in Judaic Studies
Brown University

THE BIBLE
IN THE
EARLY MIDDLE AGES

by
Robert E. McNally, S.J.

WAGGONER LIBRARY
DISCARD

MACKEY LIBRARY
TREVECCA NAZARENE COLLEGE

Scholars Press
Atlanta, Georgia

THE BIBLE
IN THE
EARLY MIDDLE AGES

by
Robert E. McNally, S.J.

© 1959
The Newman Press

Scholars Press Reprint, 1986

Reprinted by permission
of the New York Province
of the Society of Jesus

Library of Congress Cataloging in Publication Data

McNally, Robert E.
   The Bible in the early Middle Ages.

   (Scholars Press reprints and translations series)
   Reprint. Originally published: Westminister, Md. :
Newman Press, c1959.
   Bibliography: p.
   Includes index.
   1. Bible—Criticism, interpretation, etc.—History—
Middle Ages, 600-1500. I.Title. II. Series.
BS500.M36   1985   220.7'09'021   85-11897
ISBN 0-89130-912-8 (alk. paper)

Printed in the United States of America
on acid-free paper

★ Contents ★

The Bible in the Early
Middle Ages

I

The Study of the Bible
in the Early Middle Ages

★ Introduction ★

THE HISTORY of the Bible in the Early Middle Ages is the history of the Church's efforts to preserve and transmit Holy Scripture, God's inspired word. This intellectual process, in conformity with the laws of history, takes place at every moment in the life of the Church. Its most fundamental and concrete expression is the text of the Bible itself and the commentaries written on it — monuments to the Church's interpretation and understanding of Scripture at each stage of her existence. The subject matter of this paper deals with only a small segment of this vast literature: those Bible commentaries which were written in Latin in the years between 650 and 1000, a period of decadence, confusion, and transition in the history of Western theology.

In the midst of the great social, economic, military, and cultural upheavals which created the medieval world, the Church's understanding of Scripture remained static, traditional, and conservative. It was her natural response to a changing world, which was insecure in its cultural institutions and unable to create a new intellectual life. The old Roman civilization was dying. The new Christian world had not yet come fully into being. In this period of acute transition, in this cultural crisis of the Early Middle Ages, the Church held tenaciously to the text of Scripture and to the works of the Fathers as the key which would unlock the great mysteries of God's inspired word.

The historian of dogma will neither correctly evaluate

[5]

nor fully understand the biblical literature of this period (650–1000), if 'he neglects the many contemporary complexities which influenced it. The religious life, the ascetical ideals, the library system, the theological education, the monastic scriptoria, the illuminated manuscripts, the Latin text of the Bible, the patristic literature, and other similar factors are important elements in the study of the medieval interpretation of Scripture. The ethos of the early medieval Bible commentaries depends on a manifold number of viewpoints and can only be discovered in the cadre of many complex relationships.

This paper in no wise pretends to be a complete and exhaustive treatment of all the problems which are posed by a study of the Bible commentaries of the Middle Ages. It only aims at a presentation of some of the more interesting aspects of the medieval Bible with a general discussion of some related problems. I have not attempted here either to answer all questions or to solve all problems. Nor have I tried to be complete in listing all authors and all bibliography or in citing all instances and all sources. My intent is merely to draw attention to these questions, to stimulate interest in this field, and to hope that others will go further in handling these themes.

★ 1 ★

The Bible in the Middle Ages

By far the most influential book in the Middle Ages was the Bible, translated by St. Jerome into Latin and known throughout Europe as the *Vulgata latina*. The religious and cultural influences of this work are clearly found in every remnant of medieval life that has come down to us. The statuary of the French Gothic cathedrals, especially the Royal Porch of Chartres, is a concrete expression of the Bible in stone, an example of how thoroughly biblical themes influenced the plastic art of the medieval world. The same dominating influence of the Bible is seen in the reverential splendor reflected in the monumental illuminated manuscripts of the Bible. It would be hard to overestimate the artistic influence of Scripture in the esthetic formation of the artists of the Book of Kells (s. viii-ix) or the Bamberg Apocalypse (*ca.* 1000). And the importance of illuminated Bible codices for the subsequent development of Western art is proved through the considerable influence of the Utrecht Psalter (*ca.* 800). Important for the art of the Middle Ages is the influence of the illuminated Bible manuscript on plastic art. The clearest example that can be cited here is the famous Saint-Sever manuscript of the *Com-*

mentary on the Apocalypse of Beatus of Liébana (d. 798). The art of the stained-glass window also shows the influence of biblical themes. At Chartres the artist presents the genealogy of Christ in the famous rose window which represents the Tree of Jesse, and in the Cathedral of Bourges the Apocalypse window is more of a Bible commentary than a simple illustration.

The Bible not only brought into existence works of art by inspiring artistic themes, but its language, the Latin of the *Vulgata,* heavily influenced the style and vocabulary of much medieval literature; for the medieval writer was heir not only to the tradition of Latin antiquity but more especially to the *Vulgata latina;* and he was thoroughly aware that Latin was one of the *tres linguae sacrae* in which Christ's kingship had been proclaimed on the cross. More important than even the linguistic aspect of the Bible's influence on medieval literature is its spiritual influence, which is clearly expressed by the historical writers in their biblical concept of history.

The most vital influence of the Bible was on the liturgy, the center of medieval life; and the center of the liturgy was the monastery. The liturgy, the public act of Christian worship, in itself an artistic gem, is solidly founded on the Bible. The monastic liturgy included both *Missarum solemnia* and *opus Dei.* Both teach the word of God in word and symbol and both formed an essential part of monastic life. It was the monk's vocation to serve God through active participation in the liturgy and to make his daily life a continuation of its charity and beauty. The whole monastic tradition assigned to Holy Scripture as God's revealed word a supreme place. The monastic scriptoria, which produced the great illuminated Bible codices, are proof of the superlative reverence with which the *sacra pagina* was surrounded.

But within the monastery the Bible was also a *regula vivendi*. It was God's supreme directive guiding the monk along the *via regia* to his heavenly homeland. This principle is clearly enunciated in St. Benedict's Rule (chap. 73): "For what page or what saying of the divinely inspired books of the Old and New Testament is not a most correct rule of human life?" The Bible was, therefore, in monastic circles not only a source of truth but also a source book of morality which proposed to the monk the virtues to be acquired in his religious life. The fourth chapter of St. Benedict's Rule presents a list of monastic virtues, derived from the Bible, which the monk is to acquire and exercise.

The prayer of St. Benedict is constructed on the Bible, especially on the Psalms. The monastic *lectio divina,* originally designating Holy Scripture itself, came later to be synonymous with the act of reading it. This sacred reading was a religious experience, involving such careful meditation on the words of the text that they became permanently imprinted on the mind and spirit. The result of long years of this monastic prayer was a total interior saturation with the words and ideas of Scripture. The *lectio divina* was the foundation and the beginning of all monastic *meditatio* and *contemplatio,* just as at a later date it would be the foundation and beginning of all *quaestio* and *disputatio.* Just as Scholasticism was orientated towards *scientia scripturarum,* so was monasticism orientated towards *sapientia scripturarum.*

All monastic education, therefore, was directed towards understanding the Holy Scriptures, in which the triad, prayer, perfection, and service of God, was rooted. The exigencies of this "school of the Lord's service" called forth a whole series of Bible commentaries, which reach from the earliest days of Western monasticism to Reformation times. The greater number of these biblical works, especially before 1000, are of a spiritual rather than a scientific character. They were written mainly to illustrate liturgical texts or to interpret the *sacra pagina* in such wise as to make it more easily a subject of contemplation. Nowhere do we find the scientific techniques of Scholastic commentators and rarely do we find the element of contention and controversy. All of these early commentaries represent different stages and levels of learning, different views and purposes in the life of the Church. All of them are of the utmost value for establishing the character of Christian tradition. In the breadth of piety and understanding which we find in them we are introduced into a distant world—stranger to us than the world of the Latin Fathers—in which the theology of the Scholastics was in its hour of birth.

★ 2 ★

Bibliotheca and Scriptorium

Biblical exegesis in the pre-Scholastic period was dominated by an inordinate reverence for the antiquity and authority of the writings of the Greek and Latin Fathers of
the Church. According to the norm of St. Vincent of Lerins
(d. 450), expressed in the *Commonitorium,* antiquity and
authority were two of the qualities involved in the concept
of Father of the Church. These two qualities made the
strongest appeal to the early medieval scholar, whose whole
understanding of history and progress was deeply rooted
in traditionalism. It was normal to look backward into
Christian antiquity to find the answers to the questions of
the moment. If the question were biblical, then the answer
must be found in the writings of the exegetes of the patristic period. Almost all the Bible exegesis of the years 650–
1000 is marked by a rigid adherence to the interpretations
of the Greek and especially the Latin Fathers of the
Church, whose antiquity and authority commanded respect. The patristic exegesis was accepted reverently by the
early medieval theologians in conformity with their static
concept of tradition.

The whole intellectual life of the monastic schools was

molded in respect for tradition. The monk's mentality was essentially formed by a twofold influence: ascetically by the traditions of the Fathers of the Desert, theologically by the traditions of the Fathers of the Church. The Rule of St. Benedict (chap. 73) teaches that all monastic observance should be constructed on this double foundation: "But, for the man who would hasten to the perfection of the monastic life, there is the teaching of the holy Fathers, by observing which a man ascends to the height of perfection. . . . Or what book of the holy Catholic Fathers is not manifestly devoted to teaching us the straight road to our Creator?" This reverence for tradition which the Rule of St. Benedict inculcated upon his monks prepared them to accept the authority of the Fathers of the Desert as well as the Fathers of the Church as decisive authorities in both their spiritual and their intellectual life. It is not surprising that their commentaries on Holy Scripture, the fruit of their intellectual activity, are so markedly conservative and traditional in spirit and content.

But even apart from the ascetical Rule of St. Benedict, the same approach to Christian antiquity and the Fathers of the Church is found in Cassiodorus' (d. 580) *Introduction to Divine and Human Readings,* a book of the widest influence in the intellectual life of Western monasticism. In his treatment of Christian historians (chap. 17) he remarks: "It is difficult to state how frequently [the Fathers] effectually open up the sense of Sacred Scripture at most suitable points, so that, as you read along, you unexpectedly become acquainted with that which you realize you had carelessly passed over. These learned authors are excellent witnesses because of their many merits, and the ecclesiastical sky shines with them as if with glittering stars." And in his General Recapitulation (chap. 24) he writes: "Let us follow with pious zeal the paths of knowledge discovered by the labor of the Fathers. . . . Let us consider as divine beyond doubt that which is found to be said rationally in the most excellent commentators; if we should happen to find anything out of harmony and inconsistent with the method of the Fathers, let us resolve that it should be avoided."

In accord with the central place of the Fathers as the ascetical and theological authorities, monastic libraries were founded to preserve the cherished past and scriptoria were instituted to transmit it. The monastic Bible commentary is the fruit of both. It is difficult to establish the conditions under which literary activity enters the monasteries of the West, since a great number of complex factors are involved. Certainly the monks of the desert, especially Pachomius (d. 346) and his *Regula* and scriptorium, must have exerted considerable influence. It is still questionable, however, whether St. Benedict's Rule in its reference to "bibliotheca" (chap. 48) is to be understood as speaking of "library" or "Holy Scripture." But the Rule does speak of books, e.g., the Holy Scripture, the Fathers of the Church, the Conferences of Cassian and his Institutes, the Lives of the Fathers of the Desert and the Rule of St. Basil, and does make reading a part of the monastic routine. The presumption, therefore, is in favor of libraries in Benedictine monasteries from the earliest times. The *Institutiones* of Cassiodorus and his famous monastery at Vivarium, which was a very important literary center in the sixth century, are also influential factors in the development of the intellectual life of Western monasticism. Another stream of influence flowed from the British Isles, especially Ireland, from which hordes of well-lettered *peregrini* with satchels of books made their way to the monastic centers of the Continent, to Luxeuil, St. Gall, and Bobbio, which were originally Irish foundations.

St. Benedict died about 550. A generation later another monk, St. Gregory I (590–604), an ardent promoter of Benedictinism, ascended the Chair of St. Peter. Through his efforts St. Augustine (d. 604–5), the prior of St. Andrew's Monastery in Rome, was sent with fifty monks to the Anglo-Saxons, and shortly thereafter converted the Bretwalda, King Ethelbert of Kent. There is evidence to show that soon after his arrival in Kent he received "many books" from his patron in Rome, Pope Gregory (Bede, *History of the English Church and People* 1, 29). In the kingdom of Kent, the administrative center of the new English Church, a monastic school was soon established which subsequently developed into the celebrated School of Canterbury.

While Canterbury in Kent was the seat of the Church in southern England and had its monasticism and learning directly from Rome through Augustine and Gregory, York in Northumbria was the seat of the Church in northern England and had received its traditions from Lindisfarne, Iona, and Ireland. But a century after the arrival of the first Irish monks in Iona, after the difficult days of the Synod of Whitby (664), two influential monasteries, St. Peter at Wearmouth (674) and St. Paul at Jarrow (682), were founded by Benedict Biscop, who was the most distinguished monk of his day. His greatest single service to the monasteries which he had founded was the famous collection of books, both secular and profane, which he formed in the course of the several trips he made from

Northumbria to Rome. The fruit of his fourth and sixth journeys was a rich acquisition of theological books. Unfortunately there is not sufficient evidence on hand to determine what these books were, but for the period shortly thereafter we have evidence that the Venerable Bede (d. 735) was able to work in one of the finest patristic libraries in the West. A further indication of how rich Northumbria was in books in the middle of the eighth century is the library catalogue of the episcopal school of Egbert, which is cited by Alcuin (d. 804) in his poem on the saints of the Church of York.

From the time of Cassiodorus (d. 580) until the foundation of the monastery of Reichenau (724) by St. Pirminus the cultural aspects of monasticism were dark. The library of Cassiodorus at Vivarium disappeared in these days and most of the old monastic centers went into both religious and cultural decline. The most prolific Bible commentator of this period is Gregory the Great (d. 604), whose *Magna moralia in Iob* and homilies on the Gospels and Ezechiel reflect the spirit which will inspire the Bible exegesis for the next thousand years. Scholarship within the monastery fell to a low state under the heavy pressure exerted by the barbarism of Merovingian society. To appreciate the significance of this situation one need only inspect some of the cultural monuments of the sixth and early seventh centuries. The pages of St. Gregory of Tours' (d. 594) *History of the Frankish Church* show how decadent the art of Latin grammar and composition had become. During these same years, outside of the scriptoria of Corbie and Luxeuil, there is also a general decline on the Continent in the script of both manuscripts and documents. A good example is the early-eighth-century manuscript of St.

Cyprian's *De opere et eleemosynis* which is conserved in Turin in the *Biblioteca Nazionale,* HS. A. II. 2* (E. A. Lowe, *Codices latini antiquiores* 4, 444, p. 12), and a diploma from the chancery of Childebert III dated 695 (F. Steffens, *Lateinische Paläographie. Supplement* [Trier, 1909] p. 10). The same decadent state of cultural achievement is in evidence at this time in all parts of Europe outside of England and Ireland.

The important Continental centers of monastic life in the pre-Carolingian period were at Bobbio, Luxeuil, Monte Cassino, St. Gall, Fleury, Corbie, Tours, and Paris. The most significant sign of spirit and life within Western monasticism at this stage of its history is the persistent and victorious stubbornness of Benedictinism face to face with the competition of those monasteries which were still observing the harsh Irish rules. In 724 St. Pirminus founded at Reichenau the first Benedictine monastery on Frankish soil; and in the years between 747–760 Abbots Othmar and Johannes definitively introduced the Rule of St. Benedict into the Irish foundation of St. Gall (d. 645). The eighth and early ninth centuries saw an almost total victory of Benedictinism over the Irish Rule of St. Columban. The discreet charity, the moderation, the sense of permanence and of stability which St. Benedict, educated in the best traditions of old Rome, had embodied in his Rule, were well suited to prepare the monasticism of the Western world for an intellectual and spiritual renaissance.

With the rise of the Carolingians in the course of the eighth century, Europe began to possess sufficient stability, unity, and peace to be able to turn to cultural matters once again. Great monastic libraries developed and expanded, and the number of extant manuscripts which have come down to us from the eighth- and ninth-century scriptoria is very considerable. It is in this period that many monastic schools of importance were founded; and the scholars whom Charles the Great imported from England and Italy established a new tradition of learning. The manuscripts, written in the new Carolingian script, reveal a real sense of style and discipline. In the early years of the ninth century the Continental Bible schools begin to take the initiative from the Irish and the Anglo-Saxons. The illustrious biblical scholars of the second half of the Carolingian renaissance were mainly Frankish monks: e.g., Rhabanus Maurus at Fulda and Mainz, Walafrid Strabo at Reichenau, Heiric and Remigius of Auxerre, Florus of Lyons, Christian of Stavelot, and Angelom of Luxeuil.

★ 3 ★

The *Vulgata Latina*

A difficult and critical problem of the early biblical schools (650–800), a problem which the medieval world never fully solved, was the text of the Bible itself. There is no question here of the text of the Septuagint, since for all practical purposes this obscure period of Western cultural history is characterized by an almost total ignorance of both Hebrew and Greek. In the entire Low Middle Ages (650–1000) there were no more than a handful of capable Greek scholars: e.g., Hilduin of St. Denis (d. 840), John Scotus Eriugena (d. *ca.* 877), Anastasius Bibliothecarius (*ca.* 879) and possibly Bede (d. 735) and Christian of Stavelot (d. 900). The problem of the Bible text is essentially the problem of the manuscript tradition of the *Vulgata,* its history, its integrity, and its struggle for supremacy over the deep-rooted Old Latin readings, whose survival was long and tenacious. There is sufficient evidence to demonstrate the inadequate, corrupt state of the *Vulgata* text in the days before the reform of the great Emperor Charles. Like all the cultural monuments of the Western world, the manuscript tradition of the venerable *Vulgata* suffered from the corruption, brutality, and ignorance of the decadent scribes of the Merovingian age.

Perhaps the genius of Charles the Great (*ca.* 742–814) consists in his clear perception that there could be no such thing as true Christian learning, no enlightened Catholic theology, unless it were rooted and founded on an accurate text of the *Vulgata*. Every student of the history of education and the development of Christian dogma is well acquainted with the famous *Capitularia* of the Emperor Charles dealing with the restoration of studies in the Frankish Empire. In a sense, the Carolingian renaissance can be characterized as a rebirth of the Christian aspiration for biblical spirituality and biblical studies. It was a return to Augustine's idea, expressed in the *De doctrina christiana,* that the cultivation of letters should be a propaedeutic to biblical studies. Charles's intent was to develop literary education for the preservation and interpretation of the *sacra pagina*. We read in the celebrated communication to Abbot Baugulf of Fulda, composed probably between 794 and 796, a clear statement of Charles's purpose: "Whence it came that we began to fear lest, as skill in writing was less, wisdom to understand the Sacred Scriptures might be far less than it ought rightly to be. And we all know that, though verbal errors are dangerous, errors in interpretation are far more dangerous. Wherefore we exhort you not only not to neglect the study of letters but even with the most humble God-approved earnestness to vie in learning, so that you may prevail more easily and rightly in penetrating the mysteries of sacred literature." And in an earlier *admonitio* (*ca.* 789) he exhorts to textual emendation as a safeguard to Christian piety: "Correct carefully the Psalms, the notes, the songs, the calendar, the grammar, in each monastery or bishopric, and the Catholic books; because often some desire to pray to God properly, but they pray badly because of the incorrect books. And do not permit your boys to corrupt them in reading or writing. If there is need of writing the Gospel, Psalter, and Missal, let men of mature age do the writing with all diligence."

In the whole period between Isidore of Seville (*ca.* 560–636) and John Scotus Eriugena (*ca.* 810–77), the most competent master of the *sacra pagina* is the Venerable Bede (*ca.* 673–735), monk of the Northumbrian monasteries of Wearmouth and Jarrow. That the mastery of biblical exegesis should pass from Europe to the British Isles and that the greatest commentator on Holy Scripture since St. Jerome's day should be a Northumbrian is not surprising when one recalls that the Codex Amiatinus, a representative of the purest type *Vulgata* text, originated in the very circle of which Bede at that time was a member. There is even evidence to show that Bede also had in his possession Old Latin versions of Scripture and even Greek texts, certainly a Greek-Latin interlinear version of the Acts of the Apostles, the Codex Laudianus (MS Laud. Gr. 33). The monastic library, which had probably been accumulated by Benedict Biscop, was at the scholarly disposal of Bede and is a further testimony to the importance of the biblical schools of Northumbria over those of the Continent, especially in this dark period of the last Merovingians and the rise of the House of Pippin.

Mention has already been made of the official activity of Emperor Charles the Great on behalf of education in the Frankish kingdom and his personal interest in the restoration of the Bible text. The most effective single worker in this intellectual movement, which is known to historians of culture as the Carolingian renaissance, is Alcuin (d. 804), also from the Northumbrian circle and educated in the scholarly traditions of Egbert's episcopal school at York. This academic reformer was in a sense the first intellectual minister of Europe. His achievements in education were very important for his time; but the most valuable of his numerous works, even surpassing in a sense his institution of the Palace School and Library and his scriptorium at Tours, is his monumental revision of the *Vulgata latina.* Unfortunately we are not well instructed on the method and style which Alcuin employed in this vast work of revision. There is no indication of the extent to which he was personally involved in this work nor is there any evidence to establish the provenance of the codices according to which the emendations were made. The work was finished in time to present it to the Emperor on Christmas Day 800. In view of Alcuin's personal and official authority in the Frankish realm, this new version, executed according to the *domini regis praeceptum,* must have exerted considerable influence in the Bible schools of the West.

The work of Alcuin, however, did not introduce a standard text of the *Vulgata* into Europe. It did, nevertheless, as M. L. W. Laistner says, "arrest the progress of corruption and established a norm; those two achievements were of the utmost value." Another recension, made in the ninth century, was that of Bishop Theodulf of Orleans (d. 821). Contemporaneously with these two recent recensions and the remnants of the Old Latin versions, there existed four different forms of the text of the *Vulgata latina:* Italian (C. Amiatinus, *ca.* 700), Gallican (C. Bigotianus, s. viii–ix), Irish (C. Armachanus, *ca.* 812), and Spanish (C. Cavensis, s. ix). The early medieval biblical

[22]

scholar, therefore, was acquainted with the principal source of his study, the Bible, only through Latin translations, which were imperfect and uncontrolled.

The canon of Holy Scripture, accepted by the greater majority of medieval Bible commentators, was essentially fixed by Christian tradition. Apart from early papal and conciliar pronouncements, which may not have been known in the Early Middle Ages, the canon of Scripture was known through the *Vulgata latina* of St. Jerome as well as through the writings of St. Augustine. In the *De doctrina christiana* (2, 8, 13) Augustine presents his list of the canonical books of Holy Scripture. Later Cassiodorus reproduced it in his *Institutiones* (1, 13) together with the canon of St. Jerome. The Pseudo-Gelasian *Decretum de libris recipiendis et non recipiendis* (E. von Dobschütz, *Das Decretum Gelasianum* [*Texte und Untersuchungen* 38/4; Leipzig, 1912]), which probably originated in the early sixth century in southern Gaul or northern Italy, also contains the Augustinian list of the canonical books. The vast manuscript tradition of this decree is proof that it was well known throughout the West. St. Isidore of Seville (d. 636) is another influential transmitter of the Augustinian canon of Scripture. In his biblical works, especially in his encyclopedia, the *Etymologiae* (6, 2, 34–50), he enumerates the canonical books according to the tradition of St. Augustine.

★ 4 ★

The Apocrypha

The traces of the apocryphal literature which occur in the early medieval Bible commentaries require some explanation here, since the Apocrypha influenced the exegesis of Scripture. Despite the condemnation of these works by Christian antiquity, their influence persisted well into the Middle Ages, especially in Insular circles. The Church's rejection of the Apocrypha was known to the biblical schools through the above-mentioned *Decretum Gelasianum,* which characterizes them as heretical and schismatical works which "the apostolic, Roman, Catholic Church in no wise accepts," works which Catholics are to avoid. The paraphrase of this same *Decretum* which is found in the Irish *Liber de numeris* speaks of them as books "not to be copied or read or received in the Catholic Church." Yet this same paraphrase places the two pseudepigraphical Books of Maccabees 3–4, together with the two canonical Books of Maccabees 1–2, in the canon of Scripture, that is, with those books "which are to be copied, read, and received in the Catholic Church" (E. von Dobschütz, *op. cit.,* p. 66)!

Research has not yet been able to establish a definitive

list of the Apocrypha which were read in the medieval Bible schools nor has it been able to show in what manner the medieval commentators became acquainted with these spurious works. A. Siegmund (*Die Überlieferung der griechischen christlichen Literatur* [Munich, 1949] pp. 33–48) has presented ample evidence to prove that there were numerous Latin translations of the Apocrypha current in the Early Middle Ages. But in addition to the literary tradition there was undoubtedly an oral tradition which kept alive certain of the more fantastic aspects of the Apocrypha. Frequently it is impossible to determine whether the influence is based on a literary or oral tradition. A careful study of the occurrence of the apocryphal literature as source material seems to indicate that the Bible commentators used it mainly to supply inconsequential, imaginative details and almost never to displace the traditionally Christian sense of Scripture.

The four following examples, which occur frequently in medieval Bible commentaries, especially those of Insular origin, are typical of the influence which these legendary works exerted upon medieval exegesis. In the *Hexaemeron* (*PL* 91, 78C) of the Venerable Bede we find the mystical derivation of the name Adam from the initial letters of the four corners of the world: "A et D, et A, et M, a quibus litteris et quattuor orbis plagae, cum Graecis nominantur, initium sumunt. Vocatur namque apud eos Anatole oriens, Dysis occidens, Arctos septentrio, Mesembria meridies." The same derivation is to be found in so many seventh- and eighth-century Irish works that it has become almost a characteristic of Irish Bible exegesis. A variant of the same idea is the derivation of Adam's name from the four earth stars. Ultimately both interpretations go back to the pseudepigraphical *Book of the Secrets of Enoch* (R. H. Charles, *The Apocrypha and Pseudepigrapha of the Old Testament 2: Pseudepigrapha* [Oxford, 1913] 30, 13–15, p. 449), though in all probability the actual link between the Middle Ages and the Jewish Apocrypha is Augustine, who employs this derivation more than once, e.g., *Tractatus 10 in Iohannis evangelium* 2, 12 (*PL* 35, 1473) and *In psalmum 95, Enarratio 15* (*PL* 37, 1236).

Another theme from the Apocrypha is the cosmographical idea that there are seven heavens. A good example is found in the unpublished portion of the *Liber de numeris* (*ca.* 750) (R. E. McNally, S.J., *Der irische Liber de numeris* [Munich, 1957] p. 122), which originated in the Salzburg circle of St. Virgilius. The author names the seven heavens: "air, ether, olympus, firmament, fiery heaven, heaven of the angels, heaven of the Trinity." The source is clearly the *Book of the Secrets of Enoch* (R. H. Charles, *op. cit.,* pp. 432–42, 448), though there is no proof of immediate and direct dependence. There are a manifold number of both Old Irish and Hiberno-Latin works in which the same theme, borrowed from the Book of Enoch, recurs. Like the above-mentioned tetragrammaton of Adam's name, the theme of the "seven heavens" is an Irish characteristic. In the Old Irish Félire of Oengusso Céle Dé there is a petition to Christ the Lord of the seven heavens: "Sen a Christ mo labrai choimdiu secht mime" ("Sain, O Christ, my speech, O Lord of the seven heavens").

The *Book of the Secrets of Enoch* (R. H. Charles, *op. cit.* 30, pp. 448–49) inspired also another concept, the creation of man from seven consistencies: e.g., his flesh from earth, his blood from dew, his eyes from the sun, his bones from stones, his intelligence from the swiftness of the angels

[27]

and from clouds, his veins and his hair from the grass of the earth, his soul from God's breath and the wind. The same theme is found in one form or another in a number of theological, biblical, ascetical, and literary pieces whose provenance is in some way related to the Insular circle. The employment of the apocryphal conception of the origin of man is in no wise intended as a negation of the Catholic doctrine of creation. It is rather a subtle, picturesque way of expressing the old idea that man is in himself a microcosmos reflecting all the elements of the macrocosmos.

The ascetical and biblical literatures of both England and Ireland frequently speak of the "seven archangels" in their prayers or their interpretation of Holy Scripture. They are variously named, but the ultimate source seems to be the names contained in the pseudepigraphical *Book of Enoch* (R. H. Charles, *op. cit.* 20, p. 201): Uriel, Raphael, Raguel, Michael, Saraqâêl, Gabriel, Remiel. It is characteristic of the early medieval mentality to adopt the fantastic, apocryphal teaching of "seven archangels," a notion foreign to both Scripture and Catholic tradition, which recognize only three archangels: Michael, Raphael, and Gabriel. "Seven archangels" are also named in the Anglo-Saxon *Book of Cerne* (A. B. Kuypers, *The Prayer Book of Aedeluald the Bishop Commonly Called the Book of Cerne* [Oxford, 1913] pp. 153–54), a prayer book dating from the end of the eighth century. There is also mention of the "seven archangels" in an Irish prayer which dates from the Old Irish period. It is the *Prayer to the Seven Archangels for the Days of the Week* (T. P. Ua Nualláin, *Ériu* 2 [1905] 92–94) and invokes Gabriel, Michael, Raphael, Uriel, Sariel, Rumiel, Panchel.

[28]

★ 5 ★

Tradition and Exegesis

In a previous chapter, Holy Scripture was described as a
sacred authority which was transmitted through the activity
of the monastic scriptorium and understood through the
books of the monastic bibliotheca. The monastic library,
built on patristic tradition, provided intelligence of the
sacra pagina, while the monastic scriptorium transmitted
the text of Scripture, and together with it certain *nova et
vetera,* the new medieval commentaries and the old commentaries of the Fathers.

The new commentaries were essentially reproductions
of the old. The medieval monk stood in awe before the
patristic heritage which he had received through tradition.
He could not conceive of Scripture being understood in
any way other than *in sensu patrum,* the sense in which it
had been always understood. Exegesis became almost synonymous with tradition, for the good commentator was
the scholar who handed on faithfully what he had received.
Msgr. M. Grabmann (*Die Geschichte der scholastischen
Methode* [Freiburg im Breisgau, 1909] p. 179) has well
described this state of affairs as a process of receptivity and

traditionalism, an ultraconservatism which excluded all true progress in both thought and method.

Much of this exegesis consisted in excerpts from the Fathers arranged systematically according to categories or subject headings. These collections are technically known as *collectanea* or *florilegia patristica* and were intended as "reference books" for the biblical exegete. At times the material is grouped under questions and answers of master and disciple, an example of which is Wicbod's (d. 788) *Liber quaestionum super librum Genesis* (*PL* 96, 1105–68). Other exegetes in commenting on the different books of Scripture were content to list the various opinions or *sententiae* of the Fathers without personal observation or criticism. Frequently citations from the Fathers are incorporated into a biblical commentary without any reference to the source. This was the normal method of Rhabanus Maurus and others and poses the problem of plagiarism in medieval literature.

This is the general method, common to the early Bible schools; but there are exceptions. In the *De mirabilibus sacrae scripturae* of the Irish Augustine (*ca.* 650), a conscious effort is made by the author to apply the principles of science and criticism to the miracles of Scripture. This striking originality is exceptional for the entire period in question. John Scotus Eriugena and Christian of Stavelot use Greek in their exegetical work. But this is an isolated procedure and in no way a characteristic of the period. Both Claude of Turin and John Scotus raise a number of original, bold questions in the course of their exegesis, the former being so peculiar that his work stands outside the authentic tradition of this period. Despite these and a few other individuals, the pattern which all these Bible commentaries form is the same. It can be expressed in the well-known formula of Pope Stephen I which was current in this period: "Nihil innovetur nisi quod traditum est."

The greatest single merit of this narrow concept of the dependence of biblical exegesis on the writings of the Fathers is that it inspired a patristic renaissance, which resulted in the acquisition, multiplication, dissemination, and preservation of the works of Christian antiquity. There is evidence to prove that after the year 800 there was in the Frankish Empire a real interest in the collection and transmission of accurate patristic texts. To appreciate the value of this patristic renaissance one need only consult critical editions of the Latin Fathers to see how many manuscript traditions have their beginning in the early ninth century. This whole new intellectual movement, which was ultimately stimulated by a renewed interest in Bible studies, focused the attention of the Western theologians on the relation of Scripture to tradition. They were not aware of the meaning of the new problem which they had unconsciously posed nor did they have the method on hand to solve it.

However elementary and unoriginal the efforts of the Carolingian and pre-Carolingian exegetes may have been, their work provided the patristic texts for the later Scholastics and stimulated them to the solution of problems which had been raised in the course of the ninth century. The greatness of St. Anselm of Canterbury (d. 1109) as a theologian is in many respects to be found in his deep knowledge of St. Augustine, whom he used not as an authority to be excerpted and systematized into a *florilegium* or *catena,* but rather as the creator of a theological system which he could use to synthesize intellectually the Christian faith. His work, based on the theology of St. Augustine, reaffirms the correct solution of the problem of *ratio* and *auctoritas*. But decisive in bringing the mind of St. Augustine to St. Anselm was the Carolingian deposit of patristic manuscripts which this conservative, receptive age had accumulated and passed on as a legacy.

The other characteristic of early medieval exegetical method, the arranging of citations from the Fathers of the Church into systematic *catenae,* was readily adopted by Abelard (d. 1142) and used by him as the *point de départ* for the posing of provocative, disputed, original questions that were of considerable importance in bringing the Scholastic method into existence. The best example of Abelard's technique can be seen in his *Sic et non* (*PL* 128, 1339 ff.), where citations from the Fathers are so arranged in sequence as to bring out the problematic in the testimony of Christian antiquity. Abelard proposed to solve the polarity in Christian tradition by the use of both dialectic and philology, a method which had never been seriously employed by the Carolingians.

The development of St. Augustine's thought by St. Anselm and the evolution of Scholastic method from the *sententiae,* of which Abelard's work marks a stage, are representative phases in the growth of dogma and the formulation of theological method. Both processes know a long history, going back to the pre-Carolingian Bible schools.

⋆ 6 ⋆

The Greek Fathers

Because of the almost total ignorance of Greek in the West during the first part of the Middle Ages, the fulness and richness of the theology of the Greek Fathers were inaccessible to the early medieval Bible commentators. Though the Greek world remained a mystery to the Latin world, there is sufficient evidence to show that at least some of the biblical commentaries and theological works of the East exercised a real, though relatively minor, influence on the West. Greek thought was disseminated not only through the writings of those Latin Fathers who were acquainted with the intellectual life of the Greeks, but also through the various Latin translations which had been made of the Greek Fathers in the course of late antiquity. It is not possible to present here a comprehensive, detailed picture of the whole state of Greek learning in the West during late antiquity and the Middle Ages. My intent is only to indicate certain trends and influences which are of interest to the problem of medieval Bible exegesis.

Two of the most widely read Latin Fathers in the biblical schools of the Early Middle Ages were St. Ambrose of Milan (d. 397) and St. Jerome (d. 420), both conspicuous transmitters of Greek thought. The *Hexaemeron* of St. Ambrose reflects clearly the spirit and content of the *Hexaemeron* of St. Basil (d. 379), nine homilies on the six days of creation; and his *Commentary on St. Luke's Gospel* in ten books, a collection of sermons and discussions of an exegetical nature, is in full dependence on Origen. St. Jerome, who was in close touch with the intellectual activity of both East and West, incorporated much Greek thought, especially Origen's, into his exegetical works.

The exact extent to which the Greek Fathers were known to the Early Middle Ages in Latin translations is still undecided. The evidence shows that translations were made over a five-hundred-year period, from Jerome to Anastasius Bibliothecarius (d. 879); but no one has yet studied and systematized the evidence sufficiently to show how thoroughly these translations were known and used, though the work of P. Courcelle (*Les lettres grecques en Occident* [Paris, 1943]) is of the utmost importance in this field of research. Jerome translated portions of Origen's works, e.g., the homilies on Isaiah, Jeremiah, Ezechiel, and St. Luke. At almost the same time Rufinus translated Origen's *Commentary on the Canticle of Canticles,* seventeen homilies on Genesis, and some of the other homilies on books of the Old Testament. In the next century Cassiodorus (d. 580) and his monks at Vivarium were active in the work of translating the Greek authors. Two of the translations produced under his direction, the *Historia tripartita* and the Vivarian version of Josephus' *Antiquitates,* had considerable influence in the Middle Ages. Cassiodorus also mentions Epiphanius' translation of the commentary of Didymus on the Catholic Epistles (*Institutiones* 1, 8, 6), Mutianus' translation of the thirty-four homilies of St.

John Chrysostom on the Epistle to the Hebrews (*Institutiones* 1, 8, 3), and a commentary of St. John Chrysostom on the Epistles of St. Paul (*Institutiones* 1, 8, 15). One of the truly competent Greek scholars of the Middle Ages was John Scotus Eriugena (*ca.* 877), who translated the *Ambigua* of St. Maximus the Confessor and the *De hominis opificio* of St. Gregory of Nyssa, and whose knowledge of Greek influenced his theological and biblical writings. The last of the Greek translators of the Early Middle Ages is Anastasius Bibliothecarius in the third quarter of the ninth century, a scholar and translator, whose importance lies more in the direction of Church history than biblical exegesis.

The above brief survey indicates that the Greek Fathers are a factor in early medieval Bible study. In a very careful, systematic study of the Latin translations of the Greek Fathers which were known in the West up to the year 1200, Dom Albert Siegmund (*op. cit.*) has gathered and evaluated evidence which shows that the works of more than forty Greek writers were preserved in Latin translations in the West and that during this entire period more than fifty translators are known. The translations, however, were deficient either because of lack of skill on the part of the translator or because of lack of the proper instruments of scholarship or because of the defective state of the Greek manuscripts from which the translations were made. Even if the translations were perfect, corruptions soon crept into the text in the course of its transmission; or if the text was preserved from internal corruption, the vicissitudes of nature soon reduced it to a fragmentary state. Most of the manuscripts of the translations were scattered about the monastic libraries of Europe. There was no library which possessed all the available Latin translations of the Greek Fathers. Most libraries had to be content with a collection of excerpts. Under these conditions, no Western Bible commentator could have mastered systematically the thought of the Greek Fathers. There is no solid, unified, preponderant influence of Greek theology in the early medieval Bible exegesis.

★ 7 ★

The Latin Fathers

In the period under discussion in this paper (650–1000), the decisive element in Western theology is the Latin Fathers, undoubtedly because of the special relation of Europe to the Roman Empire of which it had been an integral part and because of the special theological relation of all Europe to Rome through which it had been Christianized. The Roman Empire transmitted Latin culture to the peoples of northern Europe, and the Roman Church gave them Latin theology. This Latin theology was the theology of the Latin Fathers.

The best known "patrology" in the Middle Ages was St. Jerome's *De viris illustribus,* continued by Gennadius (*ca.* 470) and St. Isidore of Seville. But more useful to the medieval scholar was Cassiodorus' *Institutiones,* which was not only an introduction to the Latin Fathers but also a guide for the medieval librarian. The afore-mentioned *Decretum Gelasianum* also served as a guide, an official directory not only of the canonical books of Holy Scripture but also of "the works of the holy Fathers which are received in the Catholic Church." Even a casual study of the biblical literature of this period reveals a strong dependence

[37]

on the Latin Fathers, especially on Ambrose, Jerome, Augustine, and Gregory.

Outside of the very important work of the Venerable Bede and the less important work of a few others, biblical exegesis in the late seventh and early eighth centuries reached a low point, because in a sense it was divorced from the true spirit and method of the patristic tradition. The following translation of a citation from the *Ioca mona-chorum,* preserved in an eighth-century manuscript in St. Gall (MS 908), is an example of early medieval Bible study undertaken independently of the Fathers.

Who died but was never born?
Adam.

Who gave but did not receive?
Eve. Milk.

Who was born but did not die?
Elias and Enoch.

Who was born twice and died once?
Jonas, the prophet, who for three days and three nights prayed in the belly of the whale. He neither saw the heavens nor touched the earth.

How many languages are there?
Seventy-two.

Who spoke with a dog?
St. Peter.

Who spoke with an ass?
Balaam, the prophet.

Who was the first woman to commit adultery?
Eve with the serpent.

How were the Apostles baptized?
The Saviour washed their feet.

That this simplistic Bible study was in vogue throughout the entire Middle Ages—though not characteristic of its better achievements—is proved by the vast manuscript tradition, which includes not only Latin but also Romance and Germanic manuscripts (cf. Walther Suchier, *Adrianus und Epictitus* [Tübingen, 1955]). Like the dialogues of Alcuin (M. L. W. Laistner, *Thought and Letters in Western Europe A.D. 500 to 900* [London, 1957] pp. 199–201), the *Ioca monachorum* reflects the academic method of the day, though it may be nothing more than a parody on the *disputatio* of the early medieval Bible schools.

One clear proof of the advance in culture in the closing days of the eighth century is the sudden appearance of the new Carolingian script, a hand so clear and precise that it has remained to this day the basis of our printed book. The scribes, however, who worked in the centuries which separate the Carolingian age from late antiquity had to copy from manuscripts which were frequently written in the most illegible of the pre-Carolingian hands. More often than not the exemplars were corrupt and were written in a script which led to further corruptions in the transmission of the work. The Irish and Anglo-Saxon manuscripts, though beautiful, neat, and accurate, were not well understood by Continental scribes and were in consequence another source of corruption in the patristic texts, especially since a vast number of Insular manuscripts were found on the Continent.

The following two manuscripts illustrate the difficulties involved in the preservation and transmission of the patristic tradition. Both *specimina* are concrete examples of the exemplars with which both scribe and textual critic of the Carolingian age had to work. The first manuscript, Lyons 426 (352), is a seventh-century copy of Augustine's *Enarrationes in psalmos* (E. A. Lowe, *op. cit.* 6, Nr. 773b, p. 22). The second manuscript, Bibl. Naz. F. IV, Turin, is written in the pointed Irish hand, probably at Bobbio at the end of the eighth century, and contains a copy of Theodore of Mopsuestia's *Commentarius in psalmos*. Both deserve careful study.

Much of the patristic literature, as we have already noted, was preserved in collections of excerpts from the Fathers. But here too a marked decadence is noted. The following example is taken from an Irish collection, the *Prebiarum de multorium exemplaribus,* which is contained in a Freising manuscript, Clm. 6302, fols. 64^r–69^r, s. viii[2] (B. Bischoff, "Wendepunkte in der Geschichte der lateinischen Exegese im Frühmittelalter," *Sacris erudiri* 6 [1954] 221–22):

Quare nos ieiunos corpus Domini accipimus, cum Dominus pro nobis non mane sed post caenam in vespere obtullit?

Quod significat finem mundi. Proinde non communicaverunt apostoli ieiuni, quia necesse «erat» ut pascha illud tybicum ante inpletur, et dinuo ad verum pasche sacramentum transire«t». Hoc in ministerium factum esset quod non accipiebant apostoli ieiuni. Ab universa autem ecclesia a ieiuniis semper accipitur. Sic enim placuit Spiritu«i» sancto per apostolis, ut in honorem nos Christi acciperimus prius Dominicum corpus quam caeteri cybi. Et servatur nunc ab universa ecclesia.

The highly corrupt form of this citation, scarcely recognizable as Isidore's comment on the Eucharistic fast (*De eccl. officiis* 1, 18, 2–3), is typical of the pre-Carolingian transmission of the Fathers.

One of the pressing problems, therefore, of the Carolingian renaissance was the acquisition and multiplication of good texts of the Fathers. In an admirable chapter on Anglo-Saxon "Learning and Scholarship," W. Levison (*England and the Continent in the Eighth Century* [Oxford, 1946] pp. 132–73) has shown how books came into the land of the Franks from Italy and Spain, frequently through England, and how the Irish and Anglo-Saxon influenced the development of patristic libraries on the Continent. The letter of Abbot Servatus Lupus of Ferrières to Abbot Altsig of York is typical of the Carolingian thirst for the works of the Fathers. He writes for copies of Jerome's *Quaestiones in vetus et novum testamentum,* Bede's *Quaestiones in utrumque testamentum,* and Jerome's *Explanationes in Hieremiam,* and promises to return the codices as soon as Latramnus, his scribe, has made copies of them.

One serious concern of Charles the Great was for the correction and emendation of the texts of the Fathers of the Church. In his *Epistola generalis* (*ca.* 786–800) he entrusted the correction of the "lectionaries for the nocturnal offices . . . unsuitable because written without the words of their authors and full of an infinite number of errors" to Paul the Deacon (d. 800), who prepared for use throughout the Empire not only an accurate *lectionarium,* based on the Fathers, but also a patristic *homiliarium* for use in general preaching. A standard edition of the works of Gregory the Great was made and an emendated edition of the *Regula sancti Benedicti.* There is also evidence of other new editions of the Fathers which were made at this time.

[41]

The influence of these emendations, which were the first serious attempt to produce on a large scale corrected works of the Fathers, was considerable in the liturgical, ascetical, and pastoral departments of life. But the return to the ancient Christian sources especially influenced biblical studies, which began to live again in the light of a newly emendated *Vulgata latina* and the newly corrected writings of the Fathers. It is precisely in this return to the theology of Christian antiquity that the Carolingian renaissance has its most original characteristic.

In the eyes of the Carolingians St. Augustine was the most revered of the Latin Fathers. This evaluation was in accord with the tradition of the West. In the *Institutiones* (chap. 22) Cassiodorus presents a characterization of Augustine which was of considerable importance in fixing his authority in the medieval mind: "That distinguished teacher, blessed Augustine, refuter of heretics, defender of the faithful, and victor in renowned contests, though exceptionally recondite and abstruse in some of his works, is so unusually clear in others that he is understood even by children. His clear words are charming; his abstruse words are heavily weighted with meaning." The same deep appreciation is found in every writer of the Early Middle Ages who mentions Augustine's name and work. Servatus Lupus of Ferrières (d. 862) calls him "a man of divine talents" (*Epist.* 5) and "a distinguished, delightful author" (*Epist.* 4). For Prudentius of Troyes (d. 861) Augustine is by far the most learned of all interpreters of Holy Scripture. These examples are typical of many others which could be cited. Even Charles the Great was under the influence of Augustine. In the *Vita Karoli magni* (chap. 24) Einhard tells us that Charles "was delighted with the writings of St. Augustine, especially the *City of God."* This enthusiasm for Augustine is well confirmed by the large number of manuscripts of his works, frequently preserved in the form of *florilegia* or *catenae,* which have survived from the Carolingian age.

By the year 800 Augustine, Jerome, Ambrose, and Gregory had been grouped into a special category, a tetrad of the Latin Fathers par excellence. If Isidore of Seville be added to these four Fathers, we have the names of the principal theologians whose spirit and work form the basis of early medieval biblical exegesis. It is not possible to list here all the writings of these Fathers which influenced the biblical literature of the Carolingian period, but mention can be made of a few of the more important: e.g., Augustine's *City of God* and his *De Genesi ad litteram;* Ambrose's *Commentary on the Gospel of St. Luke* and his *Hexaemeron;* Jerome's commentaries on the books of the Old and New Testaments, his letters, and his translations of Origen; Gregory's *Magna moralia in Iob* and his homilies on Ezechiel and the Gospels; Isidore's *Etymologiae* and his *Sententiae.* All these works were available to the scholar in many of the medieval libraries. Frequently they are cited directly from the work itself, though at times there is evidence that the author worked from *florilegia.* Some authors, e.g., Bede in his *Commentary on Mark,* identified their sources, while others, e.g., Rhabanus Maurus, in accord with the spirit of the time cited copiously without naming the source of their citations.

One conspicuous example of the intellectual influence of the patristic age on the early medieval exegetes is the adoption of the periodization of world history into six earthly ages and one celestial age. The idea is deeply rooted

[43]

in Christian antiquity, but it is Augustine who actually prescribed it for the Middle Ages. The theme, the *sex aetates mundi*, appears frequently in the course of his writings, especially those writings which were known in the Middle Ages, e.g., *De civitate Dei* (22, 30), *De trinitate* (4, 4), and *De catechizandis rudibus* (22, 29). But it was probably the *Etymologiae* (5, 39, 2–42) of Isidore of Seville (d. 636) and the *De comprobatione aetatis sextae* of Julian of Toledo (d. 667) which were most helpful in propagating the Augustinian idea of *sex aetates mundi* in the days before the Venerable Bede.

Almost all the biblical and historical literature of the Middle Ages stands under the domination of this concept of historical periodization, which divides the history of salvation into six ages. The first five ages are: from Adam to Noah; from Noah to Abraham; from Abraham to David; from David to the transmigration into Babylon; and from the transmigration into Babylon to the coming of the Saviour. The sixth age is the age of the world in which there is salvation through baptism. It is the "modern" world, the end phase of world history, the last age before the coming of the Lord to judgment, the age in which this world will die. The seventh age is the celestial age, in which man will enter into heavenly glory, the Lord's Sabbath, the eternal rest. This concept of the six ages of history, followed by an age of rest, is essentially an allegorical adaptation or expression of the biblical account of the six days of creation, followed by the seventh day of rest, the first Sabbath day.

Another division of world history was based on the seventh chapter of the Book of Daniel, which describes the vision in which Daniel beheld "four great beasts" rising "out of the sea . . . the first like a lion with wings of an eagle . . . a second beast like a bear . . . another beast like a leopard with four wings of a bird . . . a fourth beast, dreadful and terrible, exceedingly strong with great iron teeth . . . and it had ten horns." According to Jerome's *Commentary on the Book of Daniel* (*PL* 25, 527C–34D), the traditional interpretation of Daniel in the Early Middle Ages, the "four great beasts" represent the four great kingdoms of this earth, the Babylonian, the Persian, the Macedonian, and the Roman, which, succeeding one another in the development of history, form four ages of the world. The Roman Empire, the "beast, dreadful and terrible," now dominating the fourth and final age, will remain until Antichrist comes at the consummation of the world. With Rome all earthly kingdoms and empires will sink. History will end. Then there will be the "gathering of the saints and the coming of the victorious Son of God," and the beginning of the "kingdom of Christ which will last forever."

Both these concepts of the periodization of world history, which place the Christian theologically and historically in the terminal stage of the history of salvation, deeply impressed the medieval mind. The Venerable Bede, whose authority and influence in medieval computation was very great—in fact, exceeded by no contemporary—makes at least forty allusions in the course of his writings to the "six ages of the world." The influence of Jerome is clearly reflected in the *Chronicle of the Two Cities* of Otto of Freising (d. 1158), which, though written in the twelfth century, is still in the historical tradition of the pre-Scholastic period. The most immediate and important effect of the adoption by the medieval world of the patristic concept of history was the formation of that eschatological mentality which is characteristic of medieval historiography.

By the middle of the ninth century Catholic theology was well advanced towards a mastery of the Latin Fathers. The late Carolingian theologians, more so than the contemporary biblical exegetes, had acquired an intimate knowledge of patristic literature and an enlightened understanding of Holy Scripture as a source of dogma. The hundred years between 780 and 880 saw the first important theological controversies of the Middle Ages: the iconoclastic controversy, the *Filioque* clause, Spanish adoptionism, predestinationism, the Photian schism, and the Eucharistic controversy. The theological questions involved in these disputes demanded quick, accurate answers. A vast theological literature came into existence as a result of a century of almost constant dispute. Unlike the biblical commentaries, which remained conservative and traditional, this new literature, born of controversy and strife, threw new light on the vast, unexplored field of theology.

The writings of Alcuin of York against the Spanish adoptionists, Felix of Urgel and Elipandus of Toledo, the writings of Paulinus of Aquileia, especially his discourse at the Synod of Cividale on the historical development of the Creed, the works of Godescalc of Orbais on the nature of predestination and of Ratramnus of Corbie on the meaning of the symbolism of the Eucharist, show a real grasp of the perennial truth of Catholic tradition. Had it not been for the political, economic, and military disasters that fell upon the Carolingian Empire at the end of the ninth century, the intellectual life of northern Europe would have been able to develop more easily in the direction which it had taken. Scholasticism would probably have been born two centuries earlier, and Catholic dogma would have had a different historical evolution.

[46]

★ 8 ★

The Bible and Philology

The medieval Bible is a Latin book. To understand it one must read Latin; and to read Latin one must first learn Latin grammar. The presupposition of all Bible study in the Middle Ages is the pursuit of the *trivium,* of which grammar, "the source and foundation of the liberal arts," is an essential part. One of the first Anglo-Saxon arrivals in the Frankish kingdom, Boniface, the Apostle of Germany, was the author of a treatise on grammar. In the preface to this work he resumes an ancient tradition by insisting on the connection between the art of grammar and the exegesis of both the Bible and the Fathers (J. Leclercq, *L'Amour des lettres et le désir de Dieu* [Paris, 1957] pp. 71–73). The Carolingian revival of biblical studies began with a return to grammar. In fact, almost all the early Carolingians were grammarians. Peter of Pisa (*ca.* 780), the first teacher of grammar in the Carolingian schools, dedicated his work to Charles the Great. Paulinus of Aquileia (d. 802) also wrote a grammar. Alcuin, the great Anglo-Saxon master of the Palace School, not only introduced the best traditions of the *trivium* as taught in the School of York, but also composed a Latin grammar for the use of his Frankish students.

It is beyond the scope of this paper to discuss or even to

mention all the grammatical works, both ancient and new, which were known and used by the Carolingians. The best collection of them was made by H. Keil in his massive work, *Grammatici latini* (4 vols., Leipzig, 1864). The Early Middle Ages relied especially on the *Ars maior* and the *Ars minor* of Donatus (*ca.* 360), the venerable teacher of Jerome, and the *Institutio de arte grammatica* of Priscian (*ca.* 500). Bede, Boniface, Alcuin, and Smaragdus composed commentaries on Donatus' grammar which were well known in the Carolingian schools. The fame of the great commentary of Priscian, especially among the Irish, is attested by the four massive Irish manuscripts in which this work is preserved. Sedulius of Liège (*ca.* 848–58) commented on Eutyches, and John Scotus (*ca.* 877) on Priscian; Martin of Laon copied and tried to translate, as best he could, the Greek quotations in the text of Priscian. Clemens Scotus (*ca.* 850) composed a grammar which he dedicated to the young prince Lothair; and Erchanbert, monk of Freising, also wrote a grammar which was intended for use as a textbook.

The Carolingian exegete lacked the essential "tools of scholarship." His exegesis of the text of Scripture was the fruit of work done without the assistance of adequate dictionaries and encyclopedias. The two oldest Latin glossaries, composed in the Early Middle Ages, are the *Abstrusa* (*ca.* 600) and the *Abolita* (*ca.* 700), neither of which was intended or composed as a biblical lexicon. The Carolingian *Glossarium Ansileubi,* which relies heavily on both the *Abstrusa* and the *Abolita,* was equally incapable of offering the biblical exegete much assistance in solving his philological problems. All these works were based more on the classical tradition than on the biblical. In the period under discussion the famous *Glossa ordinaria,* once believed to have been the work of Walafrid Strabo, had not yet come into existence. In this matter, as in so many others, the Carolingians had to turn backward to the patristic tradition.

Generally the biblical schools had recourse to Isidore for the answer to their linguistic questions, especially to his *Differentiae, Synonyma,* and *Etymologiae.* The last-mentioned work was of major importance to the exegesis of the Bible. It transmitted a vast amount of accurate and useful information, etymological and philological interpretations, which unfortunately were too often interlaced with the fantastic and curious: e.g., "aliter dicta disciplina quia discitur plena" (*Etym.* 1, 1, 1); "fides dicta eo quod fiat" (*Etym.* 5, 24, 17); "nox a nocendo dicta eo quod oculis noceat" (*Etym.* 5, 31, 1). Bede offers a similar derivation in his *De temporum ratione* (*Bedae Opera de temporibus,* ed. C. W. Jones [Cambridge, 1943] p. 193), which is partly based on the *Computus Victorianus:* "Nox dicta quod noceat aspectibus vel negotiis humanis sive quod in ea fures latronesque nocendi aliis occasionem nanciscantur." In the Irish *Liber de numeris* (3, 12) we find this curious explanation of *caritas:* "Caritas, quid est? Cara res est, quia in mundo iam rara est." And it is interesting to note that the same tradition is found five centuries later in the *Carmina Burana:* "Dic, Christi veritas! Dic, cara raritas! Dic, rara caritas!" In his *Commentary on St. Matthew's Gospel,* Christian of Stavelot (d. *ca.* 880), following the explanation of Isidore (*Etym.* 16, 18, 6), derives *thesaurus* from Greek and Latin: "Thesauri nomen ex Graeco Latinoque est compositum. *Thesis* namque Graece, Latine positio auri" (*PL* 106, 1515D); and in the same commentary he explains the phrase of the Lord's Prayer, *Panem nostrum quotidia-*

num da nobis hodie. "Pan Graece 'omne' dicitur, et per
'panem' omnis substantia intelligitur quae quotidie nobis
necessaria est, quod est quotidianus panis" (*PL* 106, 1514D).

In the entire period between 650 and 1000 there were
less than a half dozen competent Greek scholars in all
Europe. So marked is the absence of Greek and Hebrew
philology from the biblical exegesis of this whole period
that it forms a negative characteristic of the intellectual life
of the time (B. Bischoff, "Das griechische Element in der
abendländischen Bildung des Mittelalters," *Byzantinische
Zeitschrift* 44 [1951] 27–55). Even the Old Irish, traditionally considered the unique masters of Greek in the eighth
and ninth centuries, possess this title without any justification from the sources, which, in fact, indicate the contrary
(R. E. McNally, S.J., "The 'tres linguae sacrae' in Early
Irish Bible Exegesis," *Theological Studies* 19 [1958] 395–
403). The manuscript remnants of this period show a child-
like imitation of the learning implied in a knowledge of
Greek. There are manuscripts which contain Greek letters,
the Greek alphabet, Greek words, the Lord's Prayer or portions of the liturgy in Greek, the *sacra nomina* in Greek.
Rarely do we find manuscripts such as the Greek-Latin
psalters of St. Gall and the Codex Laudianus with its bilingual text of the Acts of the Apostles—works which, if
sufficiently widespread, would indicate a competent
knowledge of Greek.

The Greek which enters into the early medieval biblical
literature consists for the most part of disparate words,
cited from the Latin Fathers or from various literary remnants of late antiquity. Outside of Bede's *Commentary on
the Acts,* John Scotus' *Commentary on St. John,* and Christian of Stavelot's *Commentary on St. Matthew,* there is no

serious employment of Greek for exegetical purposes. Jerome's *Commentary on St. Matthew* is one of the chief sources for the Greek exegesis of the text of the New Testament: e.g., the explanation of the passions of the soul according to the Greeks (*PL* 26, 39C, 94B); the explanation of the Septuagint text for Mt 21:9 (*PL* 26, 154B); the exegesis of Mt 21:1 (*PL* 26, 152B). From Augustine's *Enchiridion* (*PL* 40, 231) the Latin interpretation of the Greek *theosebeia* is taken. Cassian in *Collatio* 5, *De octo principalibus vitiis* (*PL* 49, 611A) provides the Greek names of the vices, *philargyria* and *cenodoxia*. Isidore's *Etymologiae* forms a veritable storehouse of Greek words and expressions and their signification in Latin. At times, especially among the Irish, Greek words are invented! Bede worked from a bilingual copy of the Acts of the Apostles in the preparation of his commentary, and in this manner was able to correct the *Vulgata* and throw much light on the meaning of the text. But no modern scholar who knows Greek is fooled by this display of Greek words and phrases that run through all the biblical literature of this period. The fact remains that the exegesis remained untouched by Greek.

An examination of our sources from the viewpoint of Hebrew leads us to the same conclusion: a rigid dependence on the patristic tradition, especially on Jerome. His biblical commentaries, e.g., on Isaiah, Ezechiel, and Daniel, rest solidly on Hebrew philology. The *Liber de nominibus hebraicis* and the *Liber quaestionum hebraicarum* present most of the derivations of Hebrew names and places which occur in medieval exegesis. But it was especially in the letters of Jerome that one found the most useful and most often quoted information on Hebrew philology: e.g., *Epist.*

20, on the meaning of *Osanna* (*PL* 22, 375–77); *Epist.* 25, on the ten names of God (*PL* 22, 428–29); *Epist.* 26, on *Amen* and *Alleluia* (*PL* 22, 430–31); *Epist.* 28, on *diapsalma* (*PL* 22, 433–35); and *Epist.* 30, on the Hebrew alphabet (*PL* 22, 441–45). These and similar patristic sources constitute the major portion of the Hebrew philology of the Early Middle Ages.

The early medieval exegetes, especially in Insular circles, revered Hebrew, Greek, and Latin in accord with the patristic teaching as *tres linguae sacrae,* endowed with a certain sacredness by reason of their special role in the economy of salvation. Grammar also contained within itself an element of mystery. For God, according to Smaragdus, revealed Himself in Scripture; and Scripture was read in Latin, which was known through grammar. Thus the *ars grammatica* stood on the first step of our ascent to the Trinity. Isidore, in common with the Fathers, taught that certain letters have a mystical signification: alpha and omega signify Christ as the "beginning and the end"; theta is the symbol of death; tau is the sign of the cross; upsilon signifies life. N. Fickermann ("Zu den alten Rhythmen," *Rev. bénéd.* 43 [1931] 313–21) has published a curious grammatico-religious tract from a Reichenau manuscript which shows how the letters of the alphabet signify and teach by their form as well as their name certain divine truths. Grammar and philology, such as it was then known, occupied a high place in education; but it never mastered nor exceeded the authority of the *sacra pagina.* "We do not follow Donatus, because we have a greater authority in Holy Scripture." In this age grammar was the *ancilla* of Scripture, as *dialectica* in the subsequent age would be the *ancilla* of theology.

[52]

★ 9 ★

The Bible and Allegory

Throughout all the biblical literature of the Middle Ages run two divergent streams of influence, the literalism of the school of Antioch and the mysticism of the school of Alexandria. The channel through which these different influences flowed into the biblical schools of the Early Middle Ages is the writings of the Latin Fathers, especially those who had been spiritually formed by the intellectual life of the Greeks. From this patristic literature, which the medieval world received from antiquity, the biblical scholar inherited principles of exegesis. The following rhyming hexameters, known in the biblical schools of the Middle Ages, sum up accurately the method and spirit of this intellectual heritage:

> Littera gesta docet, quid credas allegoria,
> Moralis quid agas, quo tendas anagogia.

Through Ambrose (d. 397) the biblical exegetes became acquainted with the somatic (literal, grammatical), psychic (moral), and pneumatic (allegorical, mystical) understanding of Scripture; through Jerome they were introduced to

[53]

a more scientific, more objective, and more historical method of exegesis. In almost every patristic work they studied, they found the text of Holy Scripture interpreted according to more than one sense. It could be understood spiritually as well as literally. The patristic work which furnished the Middle Ages with the most useful category of the biblical senses was Augustine's *De Genesi ad litteram* 1, 1 (*CSEL* 28, 3, p. 3), which provides a fourfold division: "In every sacred book one should note the things of eternity which are communicated, the facts of history which are recounted, future events which are foretold, moral precepts which are enjoined or counseled." Jerome also believed in the multiple sense of Scripture. In his *Commentary on Ezechiel* 4, 16 (*PL* 25, 125AB) he presents the four meanings of "Jerusalem": (1) the earthly city; (2) the Church; (3) the faithful soul; and (4) the heavenly city. And these divisions actually coincide with the four senses of Scripture which John Cassian (*ca.* 430–35) described in *Collatio* 14, *De spiritali scientia* (*PL* 49, 962B). The interpretation of Scripture is twofold, historical ("the facts of history which are recounted") and spiritual, which itself includes three different senses: allegorical ("future events which are foretold"), tropological ("moral precepts which are enjoined or counseled"), and anagogical ("the things of eternity which are communicated"). The allegorical prefigures the future. The tropological teaches morality. The anagogic reflects the celestial.

According to the *Formulae spiritalis intellegentiae* (*CSEL* 31, 1) of Eucherius of Lyons (d. 450–55), a work that was often used by the early medieval exegetes, all Scripture must be understood in an allegorical, spiritual sense, for "the letter kills, while the spirit vivifies." Actually

Eucherius held that the text of Scripture has three senses: (1) the literal, which contains the body; (2) the tropological, which contains the spirit; and (3) the anagogical, which contains the superior intellect. The allegorical is sometimes placed in this latter category. This division corresponds to the threefold "wisdom of this world": physical, ethical, and logical, or natural, moral, and rational. In the preface to his work he illustrates the four senses in which "heaven" may be understood: (1) literal: the sky; (2) tropological: heaven; (3) anagogical: angels; (4) allegorical: baptism.

The *Magna moralia in Iob* (*PL* 75, 513C) of Gregory the Great (d. 604), a work which was designed to interpret the Book of Job according to the literal, allegorical, and moral senses, was also very influential in the development of biblical exegesis. This original plan, however, was soon discarded. After the fourth book Gregory's main preoccupation is with the moral and allegorical. Despite his own prudent advice on the value of the historical sense of Scripture (*PL* 75, 514D–515A), it barely concerns him throughout the remainder of the work. We find the same reverence and predilection for the moral and allegorical in his homilies on both the Gospels and the Book of Ezechiel.

The same tendency is found in the writings of Isidore of Seville (d. 636), who composed a special work on the allegories of Holy Scripture, *Allegoriae quaedam s. scripturae* (*PL* 83, 97–130), and another work on the spiritual exegesis of certain important texts of Scripture, the *Mysticorum expositiones sacramentorum* (*PL* 83, 207–424), which did much to propagate the allegorical approach to biblical exegesis. Almost every commentary on the Bible which was written in the succeeding three centuries shows

[55]

some dependence on or connection with the work of Isidore.

Both the Fathers and the medieval commentators believed that the allegorical method of exegesis opened up the deepest meaning of Scripture more readily than the rigid, lifeless literal sense and that it involved within itself the highest spiritual life. According to Cassian the study of Scripture which is subsumed under *theoria* or contemplation presupposes *actualis* or purgation—an ascetical preparation consisting in the correction of morals and the elimination of vices. *Theoria,* which includes these three senses of Scripture, tropological, allegorical, and anagogical, terminates in the most profound understanding of divine and sacred truths. He who knows the spiritual sense of Holy Scripture becomes in the fixed humility of his heart like the ark of the covenant, filled with spiritual understanding, imbued with divine memories, guarded by two Cherubim, the fulness of the spiritual and historical interpretation of Scripture.

The heritage, therefore, which the Early Middle Ages received from Ambrose, Augustine, John Cassian, Jerome, Eucherius, Gregory, and Isidore inclined it to the allegorical interpretation of Holy Scripture as the correct method and spirit of understanding and contemplating God's revelation. And this inclination coincided well with the medieval desire to find in Scripture a celestial food on which the soul might feed, a food which was hidden deep under the superficial literal sense.

Smaragdus of St. Mihiel (d. 843) is a clear witness to the medieval concept of the spiritual function of Scripture. In the introduction to the *Liber comitis* (*PL* 102, 13C–14C), after describing his work as a "book filled with the flowers of allegory," he continues: "We present this little book to the diligent reader as a box filled with all kinds of delicacies. When the reader's mind shall have tasted this heavenly ambrosia, it will wisely seek out and examine in reading through the vast field of Holy Scripture the Lord's word and embrace it like a food which deifies and vivifies. By the comfort and solace of God's word may the reader live more prudently in this life and more happily in the next." And in the *Diadema monachorum* (*PL* 102, 593) he tells us that every word in Holy Scripture should be eaten, for the scriptural precepts bring back life after death and are a light for the journey through the present life.

The best and, in many ways, the most original treatment of the relation of *theoria* and *actualis* to Holy Scripture is found in the *Homily on the Prologue of St. John's Gospel* (*PL* 122, 283–96) attributed to John Scotus Eriugena (*ca.* 877). In answering the question whether St. John, who penetrated the hidden mysteries of the *Summum Bonum* and revealed to man the truths he found there, is greater than St. Peter, who spoke the words "Thou art the Christ, the Son of the living God," two types are distinguished: John, the man of "contemplation and knowledge," and Peter, the man of "action and faith." The former "rested on the breast of the Lord, which is the mystery of contemplation"; the latter "often vacillated," which is the symbol of trepid action.

On Easter morning both ran to the monument, a symbol of Holy Scripture, in which the deepest mysteries of the humanity and divinity are sealed up as if with a stone. St. John ran faster than Peter, because contemplation is sharper and swifter than action. Both entered the monument, because both ran. Peter, the symbol of faith, entered

[57]

before John, the symbol of understanding, because Scripture says: "Unless you believe, you shall not understand." Faith goes first. It enters the monument and prepares the way for understanding, which follows. In history Peter knew Christ as God and Man, and said to Him: "Thou art the Christ, the Son of the Living God." He flew high, but John flew even higher, for he knew the same Christ, God of God, before all ages begotten. Of Him he said: "In the beginning was the Word."

In his fragmentary *Commentary on the Gospel of St. John* (*PL* 122, 297–348) Scotus developed more fully his theory of biblical exegesis. For him Scripture can be divided into mysteries ("quae iuxta allegoriam et facti et dicti traduntur") and symbols ("quae solummodo non facta sed quasi facta sola doctrina dicuntur"). Mysteries are historical events which are reported in Holy Scripture. Symbols are reported in Holy Scripture but are not historical events. The tabernacle of Moses is a mystery, because it is an historical reality which is reported in the Book of Exodus. The parable of Dives and Lazarus is only a symbol, because it is without historical reality and merely related in the Gospel of Luke.

Mystery is composed of "the sensible and temporal" which perish, and "the spiritual and eternal" which endure. It is partly mortal and partly immortal. The miraculous multiplication of the five loaves illustrates the concept of biblical mystery. The Lord took the bread and blessed it. The disciples then broke and divided it. The breaking of the bread is a sign of the division of the mysteries of Holy Scripture into historical and spiritual fragments. The carnal are filled with the fragments of history, the "res gestae"; the spiritual are sated with understanding, "divini intellectus rerum gestarum." A mystery is divisible into two fragments, "letter and spirit," which are food for carnal and spiritual.

The scriptural symbol cannot be broken into fragments. It is an eternal and spiritual reality, totally referable to that theology which exceeds all sense and understanding. The opening words of St. John's Gospel, "In the beginning was the Word, and the Word was with God, and the Word was God," are a symbol. This spiritual truth, which stands outside all history and sense perception, must be accepted as a unit. The carnal must believe that a spiritual sense is contained therein, but they cannot understand it. The spiritual know the truth which the symbol signifies and understand it through their never-ending contemplation.

No system is discernible in the use which the medieval biblical commentators make of allegory in their exegesis. Certain allegorical interpretations are traceable to the Fathers, others are the product of contemporary schools, others are capricious or original. The four rivers of paradise are interpreted as the four Evangelists. The one fountain is Christ. Noah's ark represents the Church, and the parts of the ark represent the different parts of the Church: e.g., martyrs, confessors, doctors, etc. The sons of Noah are taken as those who believe in the Trinity, because they are three in number. The seven women in Isaiah who seize one man are the seven gifts of the Holy Spirit and the one man is Christ. The six jars of water at the marriage feast of Cana are the six ages of the world. The seven seals on the sealed book of the Apocalypse are the seven principal mysteries in the life of Christ. The two blind men of Jericho are the two scriptural peoples, the Jews and Gentiles. The man with the withered arm is the human race, which touched forbidden food before the coming of Christ and had to wait for Christ to find its cure.

The most common allegory is the representation of the four animals of the Book of Ezechiel (1:5–10) as the four Evangelists. The source is very probably Jerome's *Commentary on St. Matthew* (*PL* 26, 19). The man's face signifies Matthew; the lion, Mark; the calf, Luke; and the eagle, John. This allegorical representation had considerable influence not only on biblical exegesis but also on manuscript illumination, plastic art, and the stained-glass window. A striking development of this traditional and standard allegorical type is evident in the Irish biblical schools, where the allegory of Ezechiel is applied directly to Christ as He revealed Himself in His mysteries. In the Irish Pseudo-Jerome's *Commentary on the Gospel of St. Matthew* (*PL* 30, 551A) we read: "There are four symbols which designate the four Evangelists: a man's face, Matthew; a calf's, Luke; a lion's, Mark; an eagle's, John. All these our Lord Jesus Christ fulfilled in Himself. He was a man in His birth, a calf in His immolation, a lion in His resurrection, an eagle in His ascension." Smaragdus (d. 843), who may well have been Irish, presents the same interpretation in his anagogical exegesis of Ezechiel (*PL* 102, 333B). He goes even further when he interprets this passage in a moral sense, so that the lion signifies the strong in faith; the calf, the merciful in the Church; the man, the humble; the eagle, the mystic (*PL* 102, 333C).

Two deviations from the traditional understanding of Ezechiel's allegory, both from the above-mentioned Irish Pseudo-Jerome, are worthy of notice, since they contain allegories within allegories and since they are illustrative of the predilection of the Old Irish for fantasy.

Matthew, honey
Mark, milk
Luke, oil
John, wine.

And in the same passage of this work the author presents the Evangelists in a different allegorical setting:

John, heaven
Matthew, earth
Luke, fire
Mark, water.

★ 10 ★

The Bible and Theology

The medieval commentaries on Scripture which we have discussed in the course of the preceding chapters neither match the originality of the biblical theology of the Fathers nor surpass in theological significance the biblical exegesis of the Scholastics. Four factors, which dominated the approach to the exegesis of Holy Scripture, retarded theological advance. (1) The serious preoccupation with the spiritual rather than the literal interpretation of Scripture obfuscated the true meaning of the content of Christian revelation. (2) In the spiritual atmosphere of this age there is no great sense of curiosity, of serious problem posing. The Bible is more a norm for the spiritual life than a source of dogmatic theology. (3) The ultraconservatism, the excessive respect for tradition, were not conducive to the growth of new ideas and methods. The exegete was convinced of his obligation to hand on the text of Scripture and its interpretation as understood by the Fathers. (4) The absence of conflict among the biblical exegetes produced an unhealthy uniformity based on the unanimous acceptance of tradition. Dialectic had not yet seriously disturbed the peace of the Bible schools.

[63]

In reading early medieval commentaries on the Book of Genesis one notices that the same pattern of problems always forms. Was the act of creation one or many? Are the six days of creation to be understood in a natural or an allegorical sense? What was the first day of the world? Was the world immediately made, or mediately through the medium of *materia informata?* When were angels, light, and the unformed matter created? In what sense do the words, "and the spirit of God was stirring above the waters," refer to the Holy Spirit? To most of these questions Augustine had already given an answer in his *De Genesi ad litteram,* a treatise which was well known to every exegete and carefully followed. Bede, who was inclined to believe, like Basil, that Genesis required a literal as well as a mystical interpretation, attempted solutions of his own. But nowhere is there a real biblical theology, or even the scriptural basis of a theology, of the six days of creation; nor is there a theological analysis of the statement in Genesis that man is made to "the image and likeness" of God. Even the theology of the supernatural elevation of man and his fall through original sin is neglected by almost all save John Scotus Eriugena, whose excessive boldness and originality are exceptional among the Bible scholars of the Early Middle Ages.

In his exegesis of John 1:29 in the *Commentary on St. John's Gospel* (PL 122, 310A–311A) Scotus develops a theory of original sin which reveals the strong influence which the Platonism of certain Greek theologians, especially Origen, exercised on him. The theory, however, found no general acceptance by his contemporaries, because it was clearly outside the Christian tradition.

The pertinent exegesis begins with the words "Ecce

Agnus Dei," which refer to Christ, the true Lamb of God, prefigured by the mystical lamb of the Old Testament. He is the Lamb of God, for He refreshes us with milk, "the simple doctrine of truth"; He clothes us with wool, "the garments of virtue"; and He feeds us with the food of His flesh, "the banquet of divine contemplation." Christ is in truth the "Lamb of God," because He was immolated for the world. "Qui tollit peccatum mundi" is, therefore, rightly said of the Lamb, who has totally destroyed "the sin of the world," original sin, the sin which is common to all human nature.

In Adam the whole human race, which had been formed to "the image and likeness of God," sinned. But this Adam is not the historical Adam, who was one man, the first man to come into this world, but the mystic Adam, who incorporated in himself all men. "For that first Adam, the one who came into this visible world before all other men, was not the only one who sinned, but all men sinned before they came into this world" (*PL* 122, 310C). The historical Adam entered the world through generation (!), which could not have happened, had he not first sinned, since human generation is a consequence of sin. The division of the human species into masculine and feminine (Gn 1:27) is the second birth of mankind, a punishment for that sin by which the whole human race offended against the law of God. This sin is, therefore, original sin, the sin which originated in the common effort of all men and which bestows on all death, concupiscence, and corruption.

Christ is the destroyer of original sin because "He takes away the sin of the world." But in what sense? Through baptism. But those baptized remain under the yoke of con-

[65]

cupiscence and are dominated by death. Baptism, therefore, must only remit the guilt (*reatus*) of original sin, since it does not destroy its effects, concupiscence, death, and corruption. Original sin is remitted now in hope, later in fact. When death is destroyed, original sin, the cause of death, will also be destroyed. The total remission of original sin, completing the work of baptism, is eschatological, for only when resurrection has annihilated death will the victory be complete and definitive.

In the theology of the early medieval biblical literature Mary occupies the central place which the venerable Christian tradition had assigned her. She is the Virgin of virgins, the Mother of God. In his *Commentary on St. John (PL* 100, 749C) Alcuin aptly sums up the faith of his day in Mary: "We must rightly believe and confess that the same glorious, ever-virgin Mary is not only the mother of the man Christ, but also the Mother of God." One of the Mariological problems of the biblical scholar was the exegesis of Mt 1:18 ("When Mary His mother had been betrothed to Joseph") in conformity with his faith in the virginity of Mary. Here he relied on Jerome's four answers to the question: "Why was Christ not conceived from a virgin who was not espoused?" (*Comment. in evang. Matth.; PL* 26, 24BC). The third answer, "that she might have on the flight into Egypt the comfort of a spouse," undergoes a gradual transformation in the hands of the biblical commentators. At first the text of Jerome is simply reproduced; then, "spouse" (*mariti*) is changed to "man" (*viri*), which in turn is omitted from the text, so that the comfort of Mary in her journey to Egypt is stated without reference to her consort. The tendency, which we see at work here, is to preserve intact the traditional concept of Mary's perpetual virginity.

The explanation of the dialogue between Christ and Mary at the marriage feast of Cana is in most commentaries based on Augustine's *Tractatus in Iohannem* (*PL* 35, 1458–67, 1951–52), which joins the text of the marriage feast to the words of Christ on the cross: "Woman, behold thy son." In the Irish *Commentary on John* of Pseudo-Jerome (*PL* 30, 597D) the words of the text "on the third day" (Jn 2:1) are interpreted as the "third law," which Bede (*In s. Ioannis evang. exp.;* PL 92, 657A) explains as the third age of the world, the age of grace. Mary signifies the synagogue, because, as Smaragdus says in his *Liber comitis* (*PL* 102, 85B), "Mary . . . persuaded Christ to the working of this miracle." The changing of water into wine symbolizes the changing of the Old into the New Testament. Water signifies baptism, wine the passion and blood of Christ. In almost all the commentaries the six jars of water are symbols of the six ages of the world, and the filling with wine is a symbol of Christ filling the law and prophets with grace and truth.

The Irish Bible commentaries are remarkable for the stress which they place on Mary's role in the work of redemption. In the above-mentioned *Commentary on Matthew* of Pseudo-Jerome (*PL* 30, 551D) we read: "Four wrought the destruction of the world: a man, a woman, wood, and a serpent. And four restored it: Christ, Mary, the cross, and the man, Joseph." The Irish *Commentary on Luke* of Pseudo-Jerome (*PL* 30, 588A) places Joseph parallel with Jesus and Mary in redeeming the world. The gloss on the text, Lk 2:16, "They [i.e., the shepherds] found Mary and Joseph, and the babe," reads "Through these three the world was healed." A striking passage in the Irish *Commentary on Matthew* (*PL* 30, 552A) mentioned above sets forth the relation between Jesus and Mary:

Mary means "Star of the Sea," because a star is sweet, while the sea is bitter. Thus it is with Mary. In the sea of this world she was among sinners like the star of the sea, because, as we know, a star leads men to port, if they follow it. So it is with Mary in this world in which Christ was born who leads all men to life, if they follow her.

And in the *Liber de ortu et obitu patrum* of Irish Pseudo-Isidore (*PL* 83, 1285), which also derives *Maria* from *stella maris,* there is a litany of praise of Mary, filled with highly poetic titles, which throw light on the place of Mary in the theological thinking of that age:

> Daughter of King David!
> Root of Jesse!
> Rose without thorn!
> Mother of the almighty Lord!
> Mother of the Sun and the Flower!
> Mother of the Lamb and the Lion!
> Mother of Light and Peace!

Then follow the titles of her maternity and virginity, her excellences and prerogatives, which are based on scriptural images and language.

In an unpublished Irish work, *Virtutes, quas Dominus dominica die fecit* (Orleans 221, p. 21, s. ix), a treatise on the central position of Sunday in sacred history, Mary's relation to all other women is likened to that of Sunday to the other days of the week, an idea which is found in Jerome (*Epist.* 29, 2; *PL* 30, 231C–33B): "Just as the Lord's Mother holds the primacy among all women, so the Lord's Day has the principal place among all the other days of the week."

[68]

The study of medieval ecclesiology must obviously be based on many factors other than the development which we find in the Bible commentaries. But the tendencies which we find there show us the nature of the problem which the historian of dogma must handle. The exegesis of the celebrated text, Mt 16:16, is typical. According to Christian of Stavelot's *Commentary on Matthew* (*PL* 106, 1396D–97D), the "Christ" of which the text speaks is the "King of Christians"; "Peter" represents obedience, because he is "Simon Bar Jona," the son of the dove (Jerome, *Comment. in Matth.; PL* 26, 121B), and firmness, because he is *Petrus*. On the firmness of the faith which he professed, Christ will build His Church; that is, Peter with all the Church is constructed and built on Christ. The gates of hell, that is, vice and heresy, cannot prevail against the Church, because he who is firm in faith has the protection and help of God. The keys which Peter receives from Christ are "knowledge and the power of discernment by which he receives the worthy into the kingdom and excludes the unworthy." The power of binding and loosing is the power of forgiving sins which was granted to Peter and the Apostles and remains with their successors in the Church. Christian concludes his exegesis with an exhortation to imitate the firm faith of Peter, his dovelike simplicity, and his constancy in overcoming temptation. Smaragdus' exegesis of the same text is equally unsatisfactory, nor does the interpretation of the important Johannine text (Jn 21:15–19) which we find in both Alcuin (*Commentary on John; PL* 100, 1000–1002) and Smaragdus (*Liber comitis; PL* 102, 387–89) substantially advance our understanding of the hierarchical nature of the Church's constitution.

★ 11 ★

Research Problems

The most elementary and basic problem in all historical research is to find the sources and to make them available to the study of other scholars. Even the slightest acquaintance with the great manuscript collections of Europe in the Vatican Library, the Bavarian Staatsbibliothek in Munich, the British Museum, and the Bibliothèque Nationale in Paris, will show that there is still a vast amount of biblical literature that has never been published, material that may throw new light on the problems discussed in this paper or confirm the conclusions that we have reached. Very few of the Hiberno-Latin Bible commentaries of the seventh, eighth, and ninth centuries have been edited, despite the important role that the Irish Bible schools played in the formation of the early Bible studies. For example, in the Staatsbibliothek in Munich is the most complete manuscript (Clm. 6296, fol. 1–201, s. ix[1], Freising) of Josephus Scotus' (d. 804) *Commentary on Isaiah*. This interesting work has been neither edited nor sufficiently studied, although the number of commentaries on Isaiah during the years 650–1000 is less than a half dozen. An edition of this work with a careful study and evaluation of the sources underlying it would be deeply appreciated and might perhaps give us new information on the early medieval concept of the Messiah. One would also like to know to what extent Josephus Scotus' work is original, to what extent it depends on Jerome's *Commentary on Isaiah*.

When one considers the importance of Claude of Turin (d. 840) in the dogmatic controversies of the ninth century, especially the boldness of his attacks on the Holy See, image worship, the adoration of the cross, pilgrimages, and the intercession of the saints, one wonders why the scholarly world has failed to supply us with a critical edition of his work. An investigation of the negative aspects of his theological thinking will doubtlessly clarify the positive side of the development of Catholic dogma, at least as it is represented in the writings of Dungal (*ca.* 830) and Bishop Jonas of Orleans (d. 844). A critical edition of the works of Claude of Turin would make possible a revaluation of his character, his importance as a theologian, and his influence on the late Carolingians. Perhaps we could definitively decide his relation to the later Waldensian movement.

The medieval scholar whose field of concentration lies within the years covered by this paper does not have the good fortune to be able to work with source material edited in critical form. Unfortunately it is through the editions reprinted in Migne's *Patrologia latina* that the greater majority of the biblical commentaries are known to us. Frequently the material which is not found in Migne is loosely scattered through a number of obscure or inaccessible periodicals or monographs. The result is a general neglect of this field, or scholarly research that is incomplete and insecure. There would be a real advance in the scholarship of biblical literature of the Early Middle Ages, if there were on hand more editions like *Bedae Opera de temporibus,* ed. C. W. Jones (Cambridge, Mass., 1943), and *Bedae Venerabilis Expositio Actuum Apostolorum et Retractatio,* ed. M. L. W. Laistner (Cambridge, Mass., 1939). Both editions are critically prepared according to the best principles of textual criticism and are valuable works for the early history of the intellectual life of the Anglo-Saxons.

I have before me at the moment the new critical edition of the letters of Pope Pelagius I, *Pelagii I Papae Epistulae quae supersunt* (Montserrat, 1956), which were edited by the late Dom Pius M. Gassó and Dom Columba M. Batlle. The work, excellent in many ways, is most commendable for the careful source analysis and commentary on the text. If the method of these two editors were applied to the medieval biblical literature, we would be far advanced towards a solution of the problem of the originality of the medieval Bible schools. The edition of Beatus of Liébana's *Commentary on the Apocalypse* by H. A. Sanders is seriously defective through its neglect of the source analysis, which would have provided much valuable information on the originality of Beatus, his education, the quality of the library in which he worked, and his dependence on the patristic interpretation of the Apocalypse. The work of source analysis must be built on critical texts and is as important to the full understanding of the work as the manuscripts are to the construction of the text.

What we have been discussing in the four paragraphs above pertains to the work of the paleographer and the textual critic, a work that should be encouraged by scholars and especially by editors, since the fruit of this endeavor is

[73]

the presentation of the sources to the historian. At this point a further series of problems presents itself which perhaps can be best solved by the specialists in the history of dogma. Many of the early medieval Bible commentators have never been investigated from the viewpoint of their understanding of Catholic dogma, or, better, their place in Catholic tradition. No one has systematically studied Smaragdus of St. Mihiel (d. 843), Haymo of Auxerre (*ca.* 865), Christian of Stavelot (*ca.* 900), or Hatto of Vercelli (d. 961). It is of the utmost importance to the formation of an accurate history of dogma that we have a series of theological monographs on these and other authors of this period, monographs conceived in terms of theology rather than philology and evaluating these writers in the light of their comprehension of the *theologia perennis.*

A large portion of the *Geistesgeschichte* of the early medieval nations is reflected in their understanding of Holy Scripture. On the basis of individual studies larger studies must be made of national groups to discover whether there is any justification for speaking of a *theologia Hibernica* or a *theologia Germanica.* Does the early Irish theology differ from the Frankish as Irish script from Carolingian? A careful, methodical study of the Irish Bible commentaries, both published and unpublished, will yield a new understanding of the cultural level of Old Ireland, its relationship to Continental Christianity, and its influence on the Anglo-Saxon, Frankish, and even Italian centers of biblical exegesis. One interesting, much discussed aspect of the theology of Old Ireland is its concept of the nature of the different states in which souls exist after death: concretely, the eternity of hell and the existence of purgatory. On the basis of Aubrey Gwynn's edition of Bishop Patrick's

(1074–1084) *De tribus habitaculis animae* (Dublin, 1955) and my own independent research of the Irish Bible exegetes of the Early Middle Ages, I believe that this question can be definitely answered in the Catholic sense of the dogmas of both hell and purgatory. If similar studies are made in this period by trained theologians, new evidence may be discovered about the dogmatic development of the privileges of the Blessed Mother, the prerogatives of the papacy, the nature of grace and its relation to liberty. By the use of this method our understanding of the meaning of Christian tradition will be greatly enriched.

In our day there is serious discussion in theological circles about the increasing need of employing historical method in dogmatic theology. It has already been proved that the application of history to theology will clarify, deepen, and broaden the theologian's field of concentration without destroying its integrity as an independent science. In the history of dogma much important work has already been accomplished, especially in the patristic period and in the period from St. Anselm onward through the Scholastics of the thirteenth century. However, the theologians and exegetes of the Low Middle Ages have not been sufficiently studied. The neglect is due perhaps to the general obscurity of the period in which they worked and to the special requirements which they demand of the researcher. The mastery of this period, because of the undeveloped state of the research, must be built on an exact knowledge of many auxiliary disciplines.

A history of Catholic dogma of the Early Middle Ages is, therefore, a desideratum of all specialists in medieval theology. There is at the moment no work which systematically and fully handles the sources, the literature, and

[75]

the organic development of Catholic dogma in the years between 650 and 1000. Works such as B. Altaner's *Patrologie* and J. Quasten's *Patrology,* in accord with the purposes of that discipline, are restricted to the literature of the patristic period, whose *terminus ad quem* in the West does not generally extend beyond Isidore of Seville (d. 636). F. Cayré's *Précis de patrologie,* which covers more than 1500 years of Catholic writers, treats the Early Middle Ages too schematically to be taken seriously. The great historians of medieval dogma, such as Msgr. Martin Grabmann and Bishop Artur Landgraf, have mainly concentrated on the development of the Scholastic theology of the twelfth and thirteenth centuries. Even the works of C. Spicq, *Esquisse d'une histoire de l'exégèse latine au moyen âge* (Paris, 1944), and B. Smalley, *The Study of the Bible in the Middle Ages* (Oxford, 1952), do not present a systematic treatment of the period which is the subject of this paper.

Patrologists and patristic theologians have done more to make the Greek and Latin Fathers of the Church known in translation than specialists in medieval theology have done for the theologians of the Middle Ages. Both the French *Sources chrétiennes* and the American *Ancient Christian Writers,* with their excellent translations of the patristic texts and throughly scientific introductions and commentaries, are admirable examples of what the medievalist can do in his own field. An attempt has already been made by the *Library of Christian Classics* 9: *Early Medieval Theology* (Philadelphia, 1957). But this is far from the standard of the two above-mentioned series, which make a real contribution to our understanding of patristic theology. It is an earnest desire and hope of all workers in the field of early medieval theology that one day a series of translations, *Medieval Christian Writers,* may be inaugurated.

In the last nine paragraphs I have tried to outline some of the problems which still await a solution. Latin paleographers, medieval philologists, and other specialists can also contribute here a series of parallel problems which arise in the same field. Much work remains to be done before our understanding of the theology of this early period can be really founded on evidence. The number of scholars prepared for work in this specialty is actually too small to do all the research that this vast subject requires.

Graduate faculties of medieval literature, philosophy, theology, and even history are the centers in which these investigations can be best completed. Doctoral dissertations can make a substantial contribution, especially if they are written under competent direction and are published in series with other related studies. The study of the Bible in the Middle Ages is neither a peripheral problem nor a side issue nor an esoteric category of intellectual life. Precisely because the Bible is the book par excellence, because it dominated and formed the cultural and spiritual life of medieval civilization, its study pertains to all branches of medieval research, to literature, philosophy, history, philology, and theology.

⋆ Conclusion ⋆

The history of the preservation and transmission of the medieval Bible, the *Vulgata latina,* the spirit and method of its interpretation, is the history of Christian tradition in one phase of its development. Perhaps no other age has revered and treasured Holy Scripture as much as the Early Middle Ages. Yet perhaps no other age understood Holy Scripture as poorly as this one. Still, the contribution of the Early Middle Ages to Christian tradition was real, though neither brilliant nor original.

The concept of Christian tradition, as the early medieval theologians understood it, was rigid and lifeless, because it was too firmly constructed on the principle that Christian antiquity in itself is an infallible authority for all things. They preserved the letter and form of tradition without developing the content and spirit. But precisely because of this rigid conservatism they were able to hand on the text of the *Vulgata* and the writings of the Latin Fathers, a heritage for which succeeding centuries are deeply grateful.

The medieval Bible was not a handbook of scientific proofs. It was a book to be read and enjoyed. The Chronicles offered the monk historical stories; the Psalms, poetry; the Sapiential books, morality; St. John, theology. The Scriptures were a mirror of virtue and truth in which all the desires and aspirations of life were reflected. It was a book of life and light. The monastic rule divided exist-

[79]

ence between prayer and work, between *theoria* and *actualis;* and it was the Bible, especially in its concrete expression in the daily liturgy, which gave life to work and light to prayer in the monk's ascent to God.

II

The Bible Commentaries
of the Early Middle Ages

⋆ Introduction ⋆

I have tried to gather here all the published Bible commentaries that were composed between the years 650 and 1000, a period of European history whose intellectual life was largely dominated by Benedictine monasticism. The commentaries, listed below, are the fruit of the biblical exegesis of this monastic or pre-Scholastic phase of the cultural life of the West. In the first part of this paper I characterized the biblical literature of the Early Middle Ages and have touched on some of the problems that arise from it. The two hundred and forty commentaries which are listed here are a monument to the culture of the Early Middle Ages, especially to its understanding of Scripture and tradition.

The material is grouped under three general headings: (1) Commentaries on Holy Scripture in general; (2) Commentaries on the Old Testament; and (3) Commentaries on the New Testament. I have noted the best edition of each commentary and have presented the more relevant literature. In no sense have I attempted to list every edition or all the bibliographical material—a work completely out of the scope of this paper.

A bibliography has been included which will serve, I hope, as a help for accumulating further literature and which will direct the reader to more detailed treatments of the problems which are involved in the study of the Bible in the Early Middle Ages. To save space I have abbreviated wherever possible. A full list of the abbreviations together with the complete titles of the various works cited is found immediately after this Introduction.

The *Repertorium* of Prof. F. Stegmüller has served as a guide for the manuscript tradition of the biblical works which are listed here. Attention is called to the fact that, in addition to the Bible commentaries which have already been published, a large number are still in manuscript form. There is also a vast theological literature which dates from the Early Middle Ages and which completes the picture of the theology of this period. I hope to handle this theme in a subsequent number of the Woodstock Papers as a complement to this study.

Though I have endeavored to be complete in my presentation of the source material, I realize that in an undertaking of this kind, where one is gathering the fragments "lest they be lost," there is always the possibility of omitting something, especially since the published material is so disorganized and imperfectly edited. I would, therefore, appreciate greatly any corrections or additions which my readers would be kind enough to make.

★ Abbreviations ★

Bib	Biblica
BS	Biblische Studien
BT	Bibliothèque thomiste
BZ	Biblische Zeitschrift
CCL	Corpus christianorum, series latina
CSEL	Corpus scriptorum ecclesiasticorum latinorum
DHGE	Dictionnaire d'histoire géographique et ecclésiastique
DTC	Dictionnaire de théologie catholique
EB	Estudios bíblicos
Herm	Hermathena
HJ	Historisches Jahrbuch
HS	Historische Studien
HTR	Harvard Theological Review
JTS	Journal of Theological Studies
MARB	Mémoires de l'Académie royale de Belgique
MBP	Maxima bibliotheca patrum
MEP	Mélanges E. Podechard
MGH	Monumenta Germaniae historica
ML	Mémorial Lagrange
PG	Patrologia graeca, Migne
PL	Patrologia latina, Migne
PLat	Palaeographia latina
PRIA	Proceedings of the Royal Irish Academy
QULP	Quellen und Untersuchungen zur lateinischen Philologie des Mittelalters
RB	Revue biblique
RBén	Revue bénédictine
RHE	Revue d'histoire ecclésiastique
SBB	Sitzungsberichte, Philol.-hist. Klasse, Berlin
SBW	Sitzungsberichte, Philol.-hist. Klasse, Vienna
SE	Sacris erudiri
SM	Studien und Mitteilungen zur Geschichte des Benediktinerordens
Spec	Speculum
ST	Studi e testi
TA	Texte und Arbeiten
TAN	Thesaurus anecdotorum novissimus
Trad	Traditio
TS	Theological Studies
TSt	Texts and Studies
TU	Texte und Untersuchungen
ZKG	Zeitschrift für Kirchengeschichte
ZkTh	Zeitschrift für katholische Theologie

[85]

★ Bibliography ★

Affeldt, W., "Verzeichnis der Römerbriefkommentare der lateinischen Kirche bis zu Nikolaus von Lyra," Trad 13 (1957) 369–406.

Bardy, G., "La littérature patristique des 'Quaestiones et responsiones' sur l'Ecriture sainte," RB 42 (1933) 14–30.

Beeson, C., Isidorstudien. QULP 4. Munich, 1913.

Bellet, P., "Claudio de Turín, autor de los comentarios 'In Genesim et Regum' del Pseudo Euquerio," EB 9 (1950) 209–23.

Beyerle, K., Die Kultur der Abtei Reichenau. 2 vols. Munich, 1925.

Bischoff, B., "Wendepunkte in der Geschichte der lateinischen Exegese im Frühmittelalter," SE 6 (1954) 189–281.

Dekkers, E., Clavis patrum. SE 3. Steenbrugge, 1951.

Denifle, H., Luther und Luthertum. Mainz, 1905.

Dümmler, E., "Über Christian von Stavelot und seine Auslegung zum Matthäus," SBB (Berlin, 1890) 935–52.

Dümmler, E., "Über Leben und Lehre des Bischofs Claudius von Turin," SBB (Berlin, 1895) 427–43.

Esposito, M., "Hiberno-Latin Manuscripts in the Libraries of Switzerland," PRIA 28 (1910) C, 62–95; 30 (1912) C, 1–14.

Flower, R., Catalogue of the Irish Manuscripts in the British Museum 2. London, 1926.

Glunz, H. H., History of the Vulgate in England from Alcuin to Roger Bacon. Cambridge, 1933.

Griesser, B., "Beiträge zur Textgeschichte der 'Expositio IV evangeliorum' des Ps.-Hieronymus," ZkTh 54 (1930) 40–87.

Griesser, B., "Die handschriftliche Überlieferung der 'Expositio IV evangeliorum' des Ps.-Hieronymus," RBén 49 (1937) 279–321.

Hablitzel, J., Hrabanus Maurus: Ein Beitrag zur Geschichte der mittelalterlichen Exegese. BS 11, 3. Freiburg, 1906.

Hablitzel, J., "Paschasius Radbertus und Hrabanus Maurus," SM 57 (1939) 113–16.

Hellmann, S., Pseudo-Cyprianus de XII abusivis saeculi. TU 34, 1. Munich, 1909.

[87]

Hellmann, S., *Sedulius Scottus*. QULP 1. Munich, 1906.

Kamlah, W., *Apokalypse und Geschichtstheologie*. HS 285. Berlin, 1935.

Kenney, J., *The Sources for the Early History of Ireland* 1. New York, 1929.

Kunstmann, F., *Hrabanus Magnentius Maurus*. Mainz, 1841.

Laistner, M. L. W., "Source-marks in Bede Manuscripts," JTS 34 (1933) 350–54.

Laistner, M. L. W., *A Hand-list of Bede Manuscripts*. Ithaca, 1943.

Laistner, M. L. W., "A Ninth Century Commentator on the Gospel according to Matthew," HTR 20 (1927) 129–49.

Laistner, M. L. W., *Bedae Venerabilis Expositio Actuum Apostolorum et Retractatio*. Cambridge, Mass., 1939.

Lebon, J, "Notes sur Christian de Stavelot," RHE 9 (1908) 491–96.

Manitius, M., *Die Geschichte der lateinischen Literatur des Mittelalters* 1–2. Munich, 1911–23.

McNally, R. E., *Der irische Liber de numeris*. Munich, 1957.

Morin, G., "Textes inédits relatifs au symbole et à la vie chrétienne," RBén 22 (1905) 505–24.

Peltier, H., *Pascase Radbert, abbé de Corbie*. Amiens, 1938.

Pez, B., *Thesaurus anecdotorum novissimus*. 6 vols. Augsburg, 1721–29.

Riggenbach, E., *Die ältesten lateinischen Kommentare zum Hebräerbrief*. Leipzig, 1907.

Schönbach, A. E., *Uber einige Evangelienkommentare des Mittelalters*. SBW 146, 4. Vienna, 1903.

Souter, A., *Pelagius's Expositions of Thirteen Epistles of St. Paul*. TSt 9, 1–3. Cambridge, 1922–31.

Spicq, C., *Esquisse d'une histoire de l'exégèse latine au moyen âge*. BT 26. Paris, 1944.

Stegmüller, F., *Repertorium biblicum medii aevi*. 5 vols. Madrid, 1940–55.

Sutcliffe, E. F., "Some Footnotes to the Fathers," Bib 6 (1925) 205–10.

★ 1 ★

General Commentaries
on Holy Scripture

1. Adrevald of Fleury (Ps.-Paulinus of Milan) [d. 878]: *De benedictionibus patriarcharum.*

    Edit. PL 20, 715–32; 23, 1375–80 (incomplete).

    Lit. A. Wilmart, "Le commentaire des Bénédictions de Jacob attribué à Paulin de Milan," RBén 32 (1920) 57–63; Stegmüller 4, n. 6324; 3, n. 3410.

2. Aileran the Wise (Airerán a n-écnai) [d. 665]: *Interpretatio mystica et moralis progenitorum Christi.*

    Edit. PL 80, 327–42. This reproduces Patrick Fleming's imperfect text (Louvain, 1667), which is based on the defective St. Gall manuscript 433 (s. ix). The correction of this text is presented by C. MacDonnell, PRIA 7 (1861) C, 369–71.

    Lit. E. Dekkers, *Clavis patrum,* SE 3 (1951) n. 1120; J. Kenney 1, n. 107, i–ii; Stegmüller 2, nn. 944–45.

3. Aileran the Wise (Airerán a n-écnai) [d. 665]: *Kanon evangeliorum.*

    Edit. M. Esposito, PRIA 30 (1912) C, 1–14; W. Meyer, "Gildae oratio rythmica," *Nachrichten von der königl. Gesellschaft der Wissenschaften zu Göttingen, Philol.-hist. Kl.* 1 (Berlin, 1912) 63–67; J. Kenney 1, n. 107 cites other editions.

    Lit. D. de Bruyne, "Une poésie inconnue d'Aileran le Sage," RBén 29 (1912) 339–40; E. Dekkers, *Clavis patrum,* SE 3 (1951) n. 1121; P. Minard, "L'Evangélaire oncial de l'Abbaye de Sainte-Croix de Poitiers. Ses pièces inédites et ses particularités," *Revue Mabillon* 33 (1943) 1–22.

4. Alcuin [d. 804]: *Carmina biblica.*

    Edit. E. Dümmler, MGH: *Poetae* 1 (1881) 287–92.

    Lit. E. S. Duckett, *Alcuin: Friend of Charlemagne* (New York, 1951); E. Dümmler, "Zur Lebensgeschichte Alchvins," *Neues Archiv* 18 (1893) 53–70; F. L. Ganshof, "La révision de la Bible par Alcuin," *Bibliothèque de l'Humanisme et Renaissance: Travaux et documents* 9 (1947) 1–20; C. J. B. Gaskoin, *Alcuin: His Life and Work* (London, 1904); A. Klein-

[89]

clausz, "Alcuin," *Annales de l'Université de Lyon,* 3e sér. Lettres, fasc. 15 (Paris, 1948); W. Levison, *England and the Continent in the Eighth Century* (Oxford, 1946); M. Roger, *L'Enseignement des lettres classiques d'Ausone à Alcuin* (Paris, 1905); A. E. Schönbach, SBW 146, 4 (Vienna, 1903); T. Sickel, "Alcuinstudien," SBW 79 (Vienna, 1875) 461–550; C. Spicq, BT 26 (Paris, 1944) 33–35; Wattenbach-Levison, *Deutschlands Geschichtsquellen im Mittelalter* 2 (Weimar, 1953) 225–36; K. Werner, *Alcuin und sein Jahrhundert* (Paderborn, 1876).

5. Alcuin (?): *Brevis expositio decalogi.*
   Edit. PL 100, 567–70.
   Lit. Stegmüller 2, n. 103.

6. Alcuin (?) (Ps.-Jerome): *De benedictionibus Iacob patriarchae.*
   Edit. PL 23, 1369–76.
   Lit. Stegmüller 3, n. 3409.

7. Candidus (Bruun) Presbyter [d. 845]: *Opusculum de passione Domini.*
   Edit. PL 106, 57–104; B. Pez, TAN 1 (1721) 239–316.
   Lit. F. Zimmermann, "Candidus," *Divus Thomas* (Freiburg) 7 (1929) 30–60; Stegmüller 2, n. 1892.

8. Defensor of Ligugé (Ps.-Bede) [*ca.* 700]: *Liber scintillarum.*
   Edit. H. M. Rochais, *Defensoris Locogiacensis monachi Liber scintillarum,* CCL 117 (Turnhout, 1957); PL 88, 597–718.
   Lit. H. M. Rochais, "Le 'Liber scintillarum' attribué à Defensor de Ligugé," RBén 58 (1948) 77–83; H. M. Rochais, "Les prologues du 'Liber scintillarum,'" RBén 59 (1949) 137–56; H. M. Rochais, "Les manuscrits du 'Liber scintillarum,'" *Scriptorium* 4 (1950) 294–309; H. M. Rochais, "Defensor et les Scintillae," RBén 61 (1951) 63–80; A. Vaccari, "Il 'liber scintillarum' del monaco Defensor," *Studi medievali* 17 (1951) 86–92; Stegmüller 2, nn. 2056–57.

9. Florus Diaconus (Ps.-Remigius of Lyons) [d. 860]: *Libellus de tenenda immobiliter scripturae veritate.*
   Edit. PL 121, 1083–1134.
   Lit. A. Wilmart, "Une lettre sans adresse écrite vers le milieu du IXe siècle," RBén 40 (1930) 149–62; Stegmüller 2, n. 2291, 1.

10. Julian of Toledo [d. 690]: *Antikeimenon libri duo.*
    Edit. PL 96, 585–704.
    Lit. E. Dekkers, *Clavis patrum,* SE 3 (1951) n. 1261; Z. García Villada, *Historia eclesiástica de España* 2, 1 (Madrid, 1932) 97–104, 159–66; F. Görres, "Der Primas Julian von Toledo (680–690)," *Zeitschrift für wissenschaftliche Theologie* 46 (1903) 524–53; J. N. Hillgarth, "Towards a Critical Edition of the Works of St. Julian of Toledo," *Studia patristica* 1 (Berlin, 1957) 37–43; J. Madoz, "San Julián de Toledo," *Estudios eclesiásticos* 26 (1952) 39–69; F. X. Murphy, "Julian of Toledo and the Fall of the Visigothic Kingdom in Spain," Spec 27 (1952) 1–27; J. F.

Rivera, S. *Julián arzobispo de Toledo* (Barcelona, 1944); V. Valina, *La doctrina escatológica de San Julián de Toledo* (Comillas, 1940); P. à Wengen, *Julianus Erzbischof von Toledo* (St. Gall, 1891); Stegmüller 3, n. 5321.

11. Julian of Toledo [d. 690]: *De aenigmatibus Salomonis.*
    Edit. G. Heine, *Bibliotheca anecdotorum* 1 (1948) 196–200.
    Lit. Stegmüller 3, n. 5324.

12. Notker Balbulus [*ca.* 912]: *De interpretibus divinarum scripturarum.*
    Edit. PL 131, 993–1004; B. Pez, TAN 1, 1 (Augsburg, 1721) 1–16.
    Lit. K. Beyerle; E. Dümmler, *Das Formelbuch des Bischofs Salomo III. von Konstanz* (Leipzig, 1857); W. von den Steinen, *Notker der Dichter und seine geistige Welt,* 2 vols. (Bern, 1948); Stegmüller 4, n. 6044.

13. Paschasius Radbertus (?) [*ca.* 860]: *De benedictionibus patriarcharum.*
    Edit. Preface, P. Blanchard, "Un traité De benedictionibus patriarcharum de Paschase Radbert?", RBén 28 (1911) 425–32.
    Lit. J. Hablitzel, SM 57 (1939) 113–16; H. Peltier; Stegmüller 4, n. 6260.

14. Pirminus [d. 753]: *De singulis libris canonicis scarapsus.*
    Edit. G. Jecker, *Die Heimat des hl. Pirmin* (Münster, 1927) 34–73; C. P. Caspari, *Kirchenhistorische Anecdota* 1 (Christiania, 1883) 151–93; PL 89, 1029–50.
    Lit. K. Beyerle; G. Jecker, "St. Pirmins Erden- und Ordensheimat," *Archiv für mittelrheinische Kirchengeschichte* 5 (1953) 10 ff.; I. Zibermayr, *Noricum, Baiern und Oesterreich* (Horn, 1956) pp. 192–211; Stegmüller 4, n. 6982.

15. Prudentius of Troyes [d. 861]: *Florilegium ex sacra scriptura* (Florilegium ex vetere et novo testamento; Instructio pro iis, qui ad sacros ordines promovendi sunt).
    Edit. PL 115, 1421–40.
    Lit. Stegmüller 4, n. 7015.

16. Ps.-Augustine (The Irish Augustine) [*ca.* 655]: *De mirabilibus sacrae scripturae.*
    Edit. PL 35, 2149–2200.
    Lit. B. Bischoff, SE 6 (1954) 273; E. Dekkers, *Clavis patrum,* SE 3 (1951) n. 1123; M. Esposito, "On the Pseudo-Augustinian Treatise 'De mirabilibus sacrae scripturae' Written in Ireland in the Year 655," PRIA 35 (1919) C, 189–207; J. Kenney 1, n. 104; W. Reeves, "On Augustine, an Irish Writer of the Seventh Century," PRIA 7 (1861) 514–22; D. W. Thompson, "Sesquivolus, A Squirrel: and the 'Liber de mirabilibus s. scripturae,'" Herm 65 (1945) 1–7; Stegmüller 2, n. 1483.

17. Ps.-Bede [*ca.* 750–800]: *Collectanea.*
    Edit. PL 94, 539–62.
    Lit. E. Dekkers, *Clavis patrum,* SE 3 (1951) n. 1129; R. Flower 2,

482; S. Hellmann, TU 34, 1 (Munich, 1909) 16; S. Hellmann, QULP 1 (Munich, 1906) 100; J. Kenney 1, n. 541; R. E. McNally, pp. 32–33.

18. Ps.-Bede: *Oratio dominica explanata.*
   Edit. PL 92, 131–32.
   Lit. Stegmüller 2, n. 1685.

19. Ps.-Bede (Ps.-Remigius of Auxerre): *Interpretatio nominum Hebraeorum.*
   Edit. PL 93, 1101–1104.
   Lit. Stegmüller 2, n. 1677.

20. Ps.-Claude of Turin (?): *Brevis chronica.*
   Edit. PL 104, 917–26.

21. Ps.-Cyprian [*ca.* 650]: *De XII abusivis saeculi.*
   Edit. S. Hellmann, TU 34, 1 (Munich, 1909); PL 4, 947–60.
   Lit. E. Dekkers, *Clavis patrum,* SE 3 (1951) n. 1106; M. Esposito, "Notes on Latin Learning and Literature in Medieval Ireland," Herm 48 (1933) 221–27; J. Kenney 1, n. 109.

22. Ps.-Isidore [*ca.* 750]: *Liber de numeris.*
   Edit. (partial) PL 83, 1293–1302; E. von Dobschütz, *Das Decretum Gelasianum,* TU 38, 4 (Leipzig, 1912) 62–75.
   Lit. G. Baesecke, *Vocabularius sancti Galli* (Halle, 1933) p. 29; C. Beeson, QULP 4 (Munich, 1913); B. Bischoff, SE 6 (1954) 221; R. Bolgar, *The Classical Heritage* (Cambridge, 1955) p. 122; D. de Bruyne, "Fragments retrouvées d'apocryphes priscillianistes," RBén 24 (1907) 319–20; E. Dekkers, *Clavis patrum,* SE 3 (1951) n. 1193; M. Díaz y Díaz, "Isidoriana I: Sobre el 'Liber de ordine creaturarum,'" SE 5 (1953) 149; R. Flower 2, 488; R. E. McNally; G. Morin, RBén 22 (1905) 509–10.

23. Ps.-Isidore [*ca.* 750]: *Liber de ortu et obitu patrum.*
   Edit. (partial) PL 83, 1275–94; G. Morin, RBén 22 (1905) 507–9.
   Lit. E. Dekkers, *Clavis patrum,* SE 3 (1951) n. 1191; Stegmüller 3, n. 5170.

24. Ps.-Isidore: *Quaestiones de vetere et novo testamento.*
   Edit. PL 83, 201–8.
   Lit. G. Bardy, RB 42 (1933) 22–23; C. Beeson, QULP 4 (Munich, 1913) 28, 33; L. Traube, *Textgeschichte der Regula s. Benedicti* (Munich, 1898) p. 107; *Vorlesungen und Abhandlungen von L. Traube* 1: *Zur Paläographie und Handschriftenkunde,* ed. F. Boll (Munich, 1920) 235; A. Wilmart, "Les ordres du Christ," *Revue des sciences rel.* 3 (1923) 312; Stegmüller 3, n. 5232.

25. Remigius of Auxerre [*ca.* 900]: *Commentaria in cantica aliquot.*
   Edit. PL 116, 695–714.
   Lit. C. Spicq, BT 26 (Paris, 1944) 51.

26. Rhabanus Maurus [d. 856]: *Commentaria in cantica quaedam.*
   Edit. PL 112, 1089–1166.
   Lit. Stegmüller 5, nn. 7041–50.

27. Rhabanus Maurus [d. 856]: *De universo* (De sermonum proprietate et mystica rerum significatione) *libri* 22.

    Edit. PL 111, 9–614.

    Lit. E. Dümmler, SBB (Berlin, 1898) pp. 24–42; J. Hablitzel, BS 11 (1906) 1–105; C. Stephenson, "In Praise of Medieval Tinkers," *Journal of Economic History* 8 (1948) 26–42; A. Vaccari, "Esegesi antigua ed esegesi nuova," Bib 6 (1925) 257, 260, 266–68; Stegmüller 5, n. 7020.

28. Rhabanus Maurus (?): *Opusculum de passione Domini.*

    Edit. PL 112, 1425–30.

    Lit. Stegmüller 5, n. 7077.

29. Sedulius Scottus [*ca.* 858]: *Explanatiuncula de breviariorum et capitulorum canonumque differentia.*

    Edit. A. Mai, *Scriptorum veterum nova collectio* 9 (1837) 159–60; M. Esposito, PRIA 28 (1910) C, 91–95; PL 103, 271–72.

    Lit. M. Esposito, PRIA 28 (1910) C, 63–65; S. Hellmann, QULP 1 (Munich, 1906); J. Kenney 1, n. 373, iii; H. Pirenne, "Sedulius de Liège," MARB 32, Lettres 4 (1882); Stegmüller 5, n. 7597.

30. Sedulius Scottus [*ca.* 858]: *Expositio argumenti Hieronymi in decem canones.*

    Edit. PL 103, 346–48.

    Lit. M. Esposito, PRIA 28 (1910) C, 63; Stegmüller 5, n. 7601.

31. Sedulius Scottus [*ca.* 858]: *Expositio in epistulam Hieronymi ad Damasum papam.*

    Edit. PL 103, 331–45.

    Lit. M. Esposito, PRIA 28 (1910) C, 63; J. Kenney 1, n. 373, iii; Stegmüller 5, n. 7600.

32. Sedulius Scottus [*ca.* 858]: *In epistolam Eusebii Caesariensis ad Carpianum de canonibus evangeliorum.*

    Edit. M. Esposito, PRIA 28 (1910) C, 83–91. Cf. the Greek text of Eusebius (PG 22, 1275–92) and the Latin text commented on by Sedulius (PL 29, 529–31).

    Lit. M. Esposito, PRIA 28 (1910) C, 63, 83; Stegmüller 5, n. 7598.

33. Sedulius Scottus [*ca.* 858]: *In prologum quatuor evangeliorum excerptio.*

    Edit. PL 103, 348–52.

    Lit. M. Esposito, PRIA 28 (1910) C, 64; Stegmüller 5, n. 7602.

34. Sedulius Scottus (?): *De psalterio latine vertendo et emendando.*

    Edit. A. F. Vezzosi, in I. M. Thomasius, *Opera omnia* 2 (Rome, 1747) 20–26; Preface, ed. E. Dümmler, MGH: *Epist.* 6 (1925) 201–5.

    Lit. S. Hellmann, QULP 1 (Munich, 1906) 95, n. 2; J. Kenney 1, n. 376; G. Morin, "Une révision du psautier sur le texte grec par un anonyme du neuvième siècle," RBén 10 (1893) 193–207; Stegmüller 5, n. 7595.

[93]

35. Smaragdus of St. Mihiel [d. 843]: *Expositio libri comitis.*

    Edit. PL 102, 15–552.

    Lit. J. Kenney 1, n. 351; A. Souter, "A Contribution to the Criticism of Zmaragdus's 'Expositio libri comitis,' " JTS 9 (1907–1908) 584–97; 23 (1921–22) 73–76; 34 (1933) 46–47; A. Souter, TSt 9 (Cambridge, 1922) 333–36; C. Spicq, BT 26 (Paris, 1944) 35–36; Stegmüller 5, n. 7695.

36. Theodulf of Orleans [*ca.* 821]: *Epilogus in libros bibliae.*

    Edit. E. Dümmler, MGH: *Poetae* 1 (1881) 538–40; PL 105, 307–8.

    Lit. C. Cuissard, "Théodulfe, évêque d'Orléans, sa vie et ses oeuvres," *Mémoires de la société archéologique et historique de l'Orléans* 24 (Orleans, 1892); Stegmüller 5, n. 8006.

37. Theodulf of Orleans [*ca.* 821]: *Praefatio in libros bibliae.*

    Edit. PL 105, 305–7.

    Lit. Stegmüller 5, n. 8006.

38. Theodulf of Orleans [*ca.* 821]: *Versus in fronte bibliorum.*

    Edit. PL 105, 299–305; E. Dümmler, MGH: *Poetae* 1 (1881) 532–38.

    Lit. Stegmüller 5, n. 8006.

39. Walafrid Strabo [*ca.* 849]: *Picturae historiarum novi testamenti.*

    Edit. M. Goldast, *Manuale biblicum* (Frankfurt, 1610).

    Lit. K. Beyerle 2, 756–72.

40. Wicbod [*ca.* 800]: *Liber quaestionum.*

    Edit. PL 96, 1105–68 (PL 93, 233–85); *cont.* PL 93, 285–456.

    Lit. G. Bardy, RB 42 (1933) 24–25; C. Beeson, QULP 4 (Munich, 1913) 129; B. Bischoff, SE 6 (1954) 246; R. E. McNally, p. 34; Stegmüller 2, n. 1654; 5, n. 8376.

★ 2 ★

Commentaries
on the Old Testament

GENESIS

1. Alcuin [d. 804]: *Interrogationes et responsiones in Genesin.*
   Edit. PL 100, 515–66.
   Lit. A. E. Schönbach, SBW 146, 4 (Vienna, 1903) 43–66; C. Spicq, BT 26 (Paris, 1944) 33–35; Stegmüller 2, n. 1085.

2. Alcuin (Ps.-Augustine) [d. 804]: *De Trinitate et de Genesi quaestiones 33.*
   Edit. PL 42, 1171–76.
   Lit. E. Portalié, "Augustin," DTC 1 (1903) 2309; Stegmüller 2, n. 1084.

3. Angelom of Luxeuil [d. 855]: *Commentarius in Genesim.*
   Edit. PL 115, 107–244; B. Pez, TAN, 1, 1 (1721) 43–238.
   Lit. J. B. Hablitzel, "Angelom von Luxeuil und Hrabanus Maurus," BZ 19 (1931) 215–27; M. L. W. Laistner, "Some Early Medieval Commentaries on the Old Testament," HTR 46 (1953) 27–46; M. Manitius 1 (Munich, 1911) 418–21; 2 (Munich, 1923) 805; Stegmüller 2, n. 1334.

4. Bede [d. 735]: *Hexaemeron.*
   Edit. PL 91, 9–190.
   Lit. M. L. W. Laistner, *Hand-list,* p. 41; Stegmüller 2, n. 1598.

5. Claude of Turin (Ps.-Eucherius of Lyons) [*ca.* 840]: *Commentarius in Genesim.*
   Edit. PL 50, 893–1048. The letter of dedication to Dructeramnus is edited by E. Dümmler in MGH: *Epist.* 4 (1895) 590–93.
   Lit. E. Dümmler, SBB (Berlin, 1895) pp. 427–43; M. Manitius 1 (Munich, 1911) 390–96; J. Martin, *A History of the Iconoclastic Controversy* (London, 1930) pp. 262–66; F. Vernet, "Claude de Turin," DTC 3 (1908) 12–19; Stegmüller 2, nn. 1949–50.

6. Ps.-Bede: *Expositio in primum librum Mosis.*
   Edit. PL 91, 189–286.
   Lit. F. J. E. Raby, "Bède le Vénérable," DHGE 7 (1934) 400.

[95]

7. Ps.-Bede: *De sex dierum creatione.*
   Edit. PL 93, 207–34.
   Lit. Stegmüller 2, n. 1652.

8. Remigius of Auxerre (?): *Commentarius in Genesim.*
   Edit. PL 131, 51–134; B. Pez, TAN 4, 1 (1723) 1–125.
   Lit. E. Riggenbach, p. 104; Stegmüller 5, n. 7194.

9. Rhabanus Maurus [d. 856]: *Commentarius in Genesim.*
   Edit. PL 107, 439–670.
   Lit. J. B. Hablitzel, BS 11 (1906) 14–15; Stegmüller 5, n. 7021.

Exodus

10. Bede [d. 735]: *De tabernaculo et vasis eius ac vestibus sacerdotum.*
    Edit. PL 91, 393–498.
    Lit. Stegmüller 2, n. 1602.

11. Ps.-Bede: *Expositio in secundum librum Mosis.*
    Edit. PL 91, 285–332.
    Lit. Stegmüller 2, n. 1648.

12. Ps.-Bede: *Quaestiones super Exodum.*
    Edit. PL 93, 363–88.
    Lit. Stegmüller 2, n. 1655.

13. Rhabanus Maurus [d. 856]: *Commentaria in Exodum.*
    Edit. PL 108, 9–246; Preface, ed. E. Dümmler, MGH: *Epist.* 5 (1898)
    394–96.
    Lit. Stegmüller 5, n. 7022.

Leviticus

14. Claude of Turin [*ca.* 840]: *Commentarius in Leviticum* (Liber informationum litterae et spiritus super Leviticum).
    Edit. (partial) PL 104, 615–20; Preface, ed. E. Dümmler, MGH: *Epist.*
    4 (1895) 602–5.
    Lit. Stegmüller 2, n. 1951.

15. Ps.-Bede: *Explicatio in tertium librum Mosis.*
    Edit. PL 91, 331–58.
    Lit. Stegmüller 2, n. 1649.

16. Ps.-Bede (Ps.-Rhabanus Maurus): *Quaestiones super Leviticum.*
    Edit. PL 93, 387–96.
    Lit. Stegmüller 2, n. 1656.

17. Rhabanus Maurus [d. 856]: *Expositio in Leviticum.*
    Edit. PL 108, 245–586; Preface, ed. E. Dümmler, MGH: *Epist.* 5 (1898)
    396–97.
    Lit. Stegmüller 5, n. 7024.

18. Walafrid Strabo [*ca.* 849]: *Epitome commentarii Rhabani Mauri in Leviticum.*

Edit. PL 114, 795–862.
Lit. Stegmüller 5, n. 8319.

NUMBERS

19. Ps.-Bede: *Expositio in quartum librum Mosis.*
    Edit. PL 91, 357–78.
    Lit. Stegmüller 2, n. 1650.

20. Ps.-Bede: *Quaestiones super Numeros.*
    Edit. PL 93, 395–410.
    Lit. E. F. Sutcliffe, Bib 6 (1925) 205–10; Stegmüller 2, n. 1657.

21. Rhabanus Maurus [d. 856]: *Enarrationes in librum Numerorum.*
    Edit. PL 108, 587–838; Preface, ed. E. Dümmler, MGH: *Epist.* 5 (1898) 397–98.
    Lit. E. F. Sutcliffe, Bib 6 (1925) 205–10; Stegmüller 5, n. 7025.

DEUTERONOMY

22. Ps.-Bede: *Explanatio in quintum librum Mosis.*
    Edit. PL 91, 379–94.
    Lit. Stegmüller 2, n. 1658.

23. Ps.-Bede: *Quaestiones super Deuteronomium.*
    Edit. PL 93, 409–16.
    Lit. Stegmüller 2, n. 1658.

24. Rhabanus Maurus [d. 856]: *Enarrationes super Deuteronomium.*
    Edit. PL 108, 837–998; Preface, ed. E. Dümmler, MGH: *Epist.* 5 (1898) 399–400.
    Lit. Stegmüller 5, n. 7027.

JOSHUA

25. Claude of Turin [*ca.* 840]: *Commentarius in librum Ioshuae.*
    Edit. Preface, ed. E. Dümmler, MGH: *Epist.* 4 (1895) 609.
    Lit. Stegmüller 2, n. 1952.

26. Ps.-Bede: *Quaestiones super Jesu Nave.*
    Edit. PL 93, 417–22.
    Lit. Stegmüller 2, n. 1659.

27. Rhabanus Maurus [d. 856]: *Commentaria in librum Iosue.*
    Edit. PL 108, 999–1108; Preface, ed. E. Dümmler, MGH: *Epist.* 5 (1898) 400–401.

JUDGES

28. Ps.-Bede: *Quaestiones super librum Iudicum.*
    Edit. PL 93, 423–30.
    Lit. Stegmüller 2, n. 1660.

29. Rhabanus Maurus [d. 856]: *Commentaria in librum Iudicum.*

[97]

Edit. PL 108, 1107–1200; Preface, ed. E. Dümmler, MGH: *Epist.* (1898) 439–42.

Lit. Stegmüller 5, n. 7031.

RUTH

30. Ps.-Bede: *Quaestiones super librum Ruth.*
    Edit. PL 93, 429–30.
    Lit. Stegmüller 2, n. 1661.

31. Rhabanus Maurus [d. 856]: *Commentarium in librum Ruth.*
    Edit. PL 108, 1199–1224.
    Lit. Stegmüller 5, n. 7032.

KINGS 1–4

32. Angelom of Luxeuil [d. 855]: *Enarrationes in libros Regum.*
    Edit. PL 115, 247–552.
    Lit. Stegmüller 2, nn. 1335–38.

33. Bede [d. 735]: *In Samuelem prophetam allegorica expositio.*
    Edit. PL 91, 499–714.
    Lit. Stegmüller 2, n. 1603.

34. Bede [d. 735]: *Epist. 13 ad Accam de Samuelis libri primi allegorica interpretatione.*
    Edit. PL 94, 697–99.
    Lit. Stegmüller 2, n. 1604.

35. Bede [d. 735]: *De templo Salomonis cap. 25.*
    Edit. PL 91, 735–808.
    Lit. E. Dekkers, *Clavis patrum,* SE 3 (1951) n. 1348; Stegmüller 2, n. 1605.

36. Bede [d. 735]: *In libros Regum quaest. 30.*
    Edit. PL 91, 715–36.
    Lit. Stegmüller 2, n. 1606.

37. Claude of Turin [*ca.* 840]: *30 quaestiones super libros Regum.*
    Edit. PL 104, 633–834; Preface, ed. E. Dümmler, MGH: *Epist.* 4 (1895) 605–8.
    Lit. P. Bellet, EB 9 (1950) 211, n. 7; Stegmüller 2, n. 1954.

38. Claude of Turin [*ca.* 840] (Ps.-Eucherius): *Commentarii in libros Regum.*
    Edit. PL 50, 1047–1208.
    Lit. P. Bellet, EB 9 (1950) 209–33; E. Dekkers, *Clavis patrum,* SE 3 (1951) n. 498; Stegmüller 2, n. 1955.

39. Ps.-Bede: *Quaestiones super Regum libros.*
    Edit. PL 93, 429–56.
    Lit. Stegmüller 2, n. 1662.

40. Rhabanus Maurus [d. 856]: *Commentaria in libros Regum.*

Edit. PL 109, 9–280; Preface, ed. E. Dümmler, MGH: *Epist.* 5 (1898) 403.

Lit. Stegmüller 5, nn. 7033–36.

41. Theodemirus Psalmodiensis [*ca.* 840]: *Quaestiones 30 in libros Regum ad Claudium Taurinensem.*

    Edit. PL 104, 623–34.

    Lit. Stegmüller 5, n. 7976.

CHRONICLES 1–2

42. Rhabanus Maurus [d. 856]: *Commentaria in libros Paralipomenon.*

    Edit. PL 109, 279–540; Preface, ed. E. Dümmler, MGH: *Epist.* 5 (1898) 422–24.

    Lit. Stegmüller 5, n. 7307.

EZRA AND NEHEMIAH

43. Bede [d. 735]: *In Esdram et Nehemiam allegorica expositio.*

    Edit. PL 91, 807–924.

    Lit. Stegmüller 2, n. 1607.

TOBIT

44. Bede [d. 735]: *In librum Tobiae allegorica interpretatio.*

    Edit. PL 91, 923–38.

    Lit. Stegmüller 2, n. 1608.

JUDITH

45. Rhabanus Maurus [d. 856]: *Expositio in librum Iudith.*

    Edit. PL 109, 539–92; Preface, ed. E. Dümmler, MGH: *Epist.* 5 (1898) 420–21.

    Lit. Stegmüller 5, n. 7038.

ESTHER

46. Rhabanus Maurus [d. 856]: *Expositio in librum Esther.*

    Edit. PL 109, 635–70; Preface, ed. E. Dümmler, MGH: *Epist.* 5 (1898) 421–22.

    Lit. Stegmüller 5, n. 7039.

47. Rhabanus Maurus [d. 856]: *Epistola ad Ermengardam Augustam dedicans commentarium libri Esther.*

    Edit. E. Dümmler, MGH: *Epist.* 5 (1898) 500–501; E. Dümmler, MGH: *Poetae* 2, 167.

JOB

48. Adalbert of Metz (Adalbert of Spalding?) [*ca.* 968]: *Prologus in excerpta ex Gregorii commentario in Iob.*

    Edit. PL 136, 1309–12.

    Lit. J. Dalstein, "Adalbert," DHGE 1, 443–44; Stegmüller 2, n. 859.

49. John the Abbot [*ca.* 940]: *Sententiae morales super Iob.*
    Edit. Preface, *Bibliotheca Casinensis* 5, 101–2.
    Lit. Stegmüller 3, n. 4130.

50. Odo of Cluny [d. 942]: *Epitome Gregorii Moralium in Iob.*
    Edit. PL 133, 107–512.
    Lit. Stegmüller 4, n. 6118.

PSALMS

51. Alcuin [d. 804]: *Expositio in psalmum 118.*
    Edit. PL 100, 597–620.
    Lit. Stegmüller 2, n. 1091.

52. Alcuin [d. 804]: *Expositio in psalmos graduales.*
    Edit. PL 100, 619–38.
    Lit. Stegmüller 2, n. 1090.

53. Alcuin [d. 804]: *Expositio in psalmos paenitentiales.*
    Edit. PL 100, 570–96.
    Lit. Stegmüller 2, n. 1089.

54. Alcuin (?) (Ps.-Rufinus: Letbertus of St. Rufus ?): *Commentarius in psalmos 1–75.*
    Edit. PL 21, 633–960.
    Lit. H. Brewer, "Der Pseudo-Rufinische 'Commentarius in LXXV psalmos' ein Werk Alcuins," ZkTh 37 (1913) 668–75; G. Morin, "Une restitution en faveur d'Alcuin," RBén 30 (1913) 458–59; A. Wilmart, "Le commentaire sur les psaumes imprimé sous le nom de Rufin," RBén 31 (1914–19) 258–76; Stegmüller 2, n. 1088.

55. Anonymous (Irish): *Commentarius in psalmos.*
    Edit. K. Meyer, *Hibernica minor,* in *Anecdota Oxoniensia,* Med. Mod. Ser. 8 (Oxford, 1894).
    Lit. J. Kenney 1, nn. 665–66.

56. Florus Diaconus [d. 860]: *Epigrammata in psalmos 22, 25, 27.*
    Edit. PL 61, 1085–86; E. Dümmler, MGH: *Poetae* 2 (1884) 535–39.
    Lit. Stegmüller 2, n. 2274.

57. Florus Diaconus [d. 860]: *De psalterii emendatione.*
    Edit. A. Mai, *Scriptorum veterum nova collectio* 3 (1828) 252–55.
    Lit. Stegmüller 2, n. 2274.

58. Paschasius Radbertus [*ca.* 860]: *Expositio in psalmum 44.*
    Edit. PL 120, 993–1060.
    Lit. Stegmüller 4, n. 6261.

59. Prudentius of Troyes [d. 861]: *Breviarium psalterii, Flores psalmorum, Collectanea psalmorum.*
    Edit. PL 115, 1449–56.
    Lit. Stegmüller 4, n. 7016.

60. Ps.-Alcuin (Italian: Nonantola ?): *De psalmorum usu.*

Edit. PL 101, 465–508.

Lit. A. Wilmart, "Lȇ manuel de prières de saint Jean Gualbert," RBén 46 (1936) 257–99.

61. Ps.-Bede: *Catalogus diapsalmatum.*
    Edit. PL 93, 1097–99.

62. Ps.-Bede: *Interpretatio psalterii artis cantilenae.*
    Edit. PL 93, 1099–1102.

63. Remigius of Auxerre [*ca.* 900]: *Diversa diversorum in psalmos praeambula.*
    Edit. PL 131, 133–46.
    Lit. C. Spicq, BT 26 (Paris, 1944) 51–52; Stegmüller 5, n. 7211.

64. Walafrid Strabo [*ca.* 849]: *Expositio in 20 primos psalmos.*
    Edit. PL 114, 751–94.
    Lit. L. C. Mohlberg, "Kleine Notizen zu einem 'verschollenen' Psalmen-Kommentar Walahfrid Strabos," ST 122 (Rome, 1947) 1–15; Stegmüller 5, n. 8324.

PROVERBS

65. Bede [d. 735]: *Super Parabolas Salomonis allegorica expositio.*
    Edit. PL 91, 937–1040 (Cf. Ps.-Rhabanus Maurus, *Comment. in Parabolas Salomonis:* PL 111, 679–792).
    Lit. E. Dekkers, *Clavis patrum,* SE 3 (1951) n. 1351; J. Hablitzel, "Bedas 'Expositio in Proverbia Salomonis' und seine Quellen," BZ 24 (1938–39) 357–59; Stegmüller 2, n. 1609.

66. Bede [d. 735]: *In Proverbia Salomonis allegorica interpretatio.*
    Edit. PL 91, 1051–66.
    Lit. J. Schildenberger, "Die altlateinischen Texte des Proverbien-Buches," TA 32–33 (Beuron, 1941) 145–49; Stegmüller 2, n. 1668.

ECCLESIASTES

67. Alcuin [d. 804]: *Commentarius in Ecclesiasten.*
    Edit. PL 100, 667–722.
    Lit. E. A. Lowe, "A Manuscript of Alcuin in the Script of Tours," *Classical and Medieval Studies in Honor of E. K. Rand,* ed. L. W. Jones (New York, 1938) pp. 191–93; Stegmüller 2, n. 1093.

CANTICLE OF CANTICLES

68. Alcuin [d. 804]: *Compendium in Cantica canticorum.*
    Edit. PL 100, 641–64 (Cf. 663–66: Epist. ad Daphnin).
    Lit. Stegmüller 2, n. 1092.

69. Angelom of Luxeuil [d. 855]: *Enarrationes in Cantica canticorum.*
    Edit. PL 115, 551–628.
    Lit. Stegmüller 2, n. 1339.

70. Bede [d. 735]: *In Cantica canticorum allegorica expositio.*

[101]

Edit. PL 91, 1065–1236.

Lit. Stegmüller 2, n. 1610.

71. Haymo of Auxerre (?) (Ps.-Haymo of Halberstadt): *Enarratio in Cantica canticorum.*

    Edit. PL 117, 295–358 (70, 1056–1106: Ps.-Cassiodorus).

    Lit. D. de Bruyne, "Cassiodore et l'Amiatinus," RBén 39 (1927) 261, n. 1; E. Dekkers, *Clavis patrum,* SE 3 (1951) n. 910; M. Manitius 1 (Munich, 1911) 50, n. 9; G. Morin, "Bérenger contre Bérenger," *Recherches de théol. ancienne et médiévale* 4 (1932) 116, n. 19; A. Vaccari, "L'Editio princeps del commento di Aimone alla Cantica e la chiave di un problema letterario," Bib 5 (1924) 183–91; A. Vega, "El comentario al Cantar de los Cantares atribuido a Cassiodoro, es español?", *Ciudad de Dios* 154 (1942) 143–55; Stegmüller 3, nn. 3065, 3079.

72. Hincmar of Reims [d. 882]: *Explanatio in ferculum Salomonis.*

    Edit. PL 125, 817–34.

    Lit. M. Manitius 1 (Munich, 1911) 339–54; C. Spicq, BT 26 (Paris, 1944) 50; Stegmüller 3, n. 3562.

WISDOM

73. Bede [d. 735]: *In Sapientiam Salomonis allegoricae interpretationis fragmenta.*

    Edit. PL 91, 1060–62, 1064.

    Lit. Stegmüller 2, n. 1674.

74. Ps.-Bede: *De Salomone iudicium.*

    Edit. PL 91, 1065–66.

    Lit. Stegmüller 2, n. 1676.

75. Rhabanus Maurus [d. 856]: *Commentarius in librum Sapientiae.*

    Edit. PL 109, 671–762; Preface, ed. E. Dümmler, MGH: *Epist.* 5 (1898) 425–26.

    Lit. Stegmüller 5, n. 7052.

ECCLESIASTICUS

76. Bede [d. 735]: *In Ecclesiasticum Salomonis allegoricae interpretationis fragmenta.*

    Edit. PL 91, 1062–64.

    Lit. Stegmüller 2, n. 1675.

77. Rhabanus Maurus [d. 856]: *Commentarius in Ecclesiasticum.*

    Edit. PL 109, 763–1126; Preface, ed. E. Dümmler, MGH: *Epist.* 5 (1898) 427–28.

    Lit. Stegmüller 5, n. 7053.

ISAIAH

78. Bede [d. 735]: *Epist. 15 ad Accam de Isaia 24:21–23.*

Edit. PL 94, 702–10.

Lit. Stegmüller 2, n. 1611.

79. Josephus Scotus [*ca.* 804]: *Epitome commentarii s. Hieronymi in Isaiam.*

   Edit. (partial) PL 99, 821–22; Preface, ed. E. Dümmler, MGH: *Poetae* 1 (1881) 149–59; H. Hagen, *Carmina medii aevi* (Bern, 1877) pp. 116–24, 216–20.

   Lit. B. Bischoff, SE 6 (1954) 234; J. Kenney 1, n. 341; Stegmüller 3, n. 5146.

80. Remigius of Auxerre (?) (Ps.-Haymo of Halberstadt): *Commentarius in Isaiam.*

   Edit. PL 116, 715–1086.

   Lit. C. Spicq, BT 26 (Paris, 1944) 51; Stegmüller 3, n. 3083.

81. Rhabanus Maurus [d. 856]: *Enarratio in Isaiam.*

   Edit. Preface, ed. F. Kunstmann, pp. 225–26; E. Dümmler, MGH: *Epist.* 5 (1898) 501–2.

   Lit. Stegmüller 5, n. 7053.

JEREMIAH

82. Odo of Cluny [d. 942]: *Collationes.*

   Edit. PL 133, 517–638.

   Lit. A. Fliche, *La réforme grégorienne* 1 (Louvain, 1924) 43–47; Stegmüller 4, n. 6119.

83. Rhabanus Maurus [d. 856]: *Enarratio in Ieremiam.*

   Edit. PL 111, 793–1182; Preface, ed. E. Dümmler, MGH: *Epist.* 5 (1898) 443–44.

   Lit. J. B. Hablitzel, SM 40 (1919–20) 243–51; Stegmüller 5, n. 7054.

LAMENTATIONS

84. Paschasius Radbertus [*ca.* 865]: *In Threnos sive Lamentationes Ieremiae.*

   Edit. PL 120, 1059–1256.

   Lit. Stegmüller 4, n. 6262.

85. Rhabanus Maurus [d. 856]: *Enarratio in Lamentationes.*

   Edit. PL 111, 1181–1272.

   Lit. Stegmüller 5, n. 7055.

BARUCH (?)

EZECHIEL

86. Rhabanus Maurus [d. 856]: *Enarratio in Ezechielem.*

   Edit. PL 110, 493–1084; Preface, ed. E. Dümmler, MGH: *Epist.* 5 (1898) 475–78.

   Lit. Stegmüller 5, n. 7056.

DANIEL

87. Rhabanus Maurus [d. 856]: *Enarratio in Daniel.*

[103]

Edit. Preface, ed. F. Kunstmann, pp, 210–13; E. Dümmler, MGH: *Epist.* 5 (1898) 467–69.
Lit. Stegmüller 5, n. 7057.

MINOR PROPHETS

88. Remigius of Auxerre (?) (Ps.-Haymo of Halberstadt): *Enarratio in 12 prophetas minores.*
    Edit. PL 117, 11–294.
    Lit. P. Glorieux, "Pour revaloriser Migne," *Mélanges de science religieuse,* Suppl. 9 (1952) 57; C. Spicq, BT 26 (Paris, 1944) 51; Stegmüller 3, nn. 3070, 3088.

HABAKKUK

89. Bede [d. 735]: *Super Canticum Habacuc allegorica expositio.*
    Edit. PL 91, 1235–54.
    Lit. Stegmüller 2, n. 1612.

MACCABEES

90. Rhabanus Maurus [d. 856]: *Commentaria in libros Machabaeorum.*
    Edit. PL 109, 1125–1256; Preface, ed. E. Dümmler, MGH: *Epist.* 5 (1898) 424–25; 469–70.
    Lit. Stegmüller 5, nn. 7058–59.

★ 3 ★

Commentaries
on the New Testament

MATTHEW

1. Alcuin [d. 804]: *In genealogiam Christi* (Interpretatio nominum Hebraicorum).
    Edit. PL 100, 725–34.
    Lit. A. E. Schönbach, SBW 146, 4 (Vienna, 1903) 78; Stegmüller 2, n. 1094.

2. Anonymous (Irish: *ca.* 750–800): *Commentarius in evangelium s. Matthaei.*
    Edit. K. Köberlin, *Eine Würzburger Evangelienhandschrift* (Augsburg, 1891).
    Lit. B. Bischoff, SE 6 (1954) 251–53; B. Bischoff and J. Hofmann, "Libri sancti Kyliani," *Quellen und Forschungen zur Geschichte des Bistums und Hochstifts Würzburg* 6 (Würzburg, 1952) 10, 99; J. Hablitzel, BS 11 (1906) 96–102.

3. Christian of Stavelot [*ca.* 900]: *Expositio in Matthaeum evangelistam.*
    Edit. PL 106, 1261–1504.
    Lit. E. Dümmler, SBB (Berlin, 1890) 935–52; M. L. W. Laistner, HTR 20 (1927) 129–49; J. Lebon, RHE 9 (1908) 491–96; A. E. Schönbach, SBW 146, 4 (Vienna, 1903) 174; Stegmüller 2, n. 1926.

4. Claude of Turin [*ca.* 840]: *Praefatio in catenam super s. Matthaeum.*
    Edit. (partial) E. Dümmler, MGH: *Epist.* 4 (1895) 593–96; PL 104, 833–38.
    Lit. E. Dümmler, SBB (Berlin, 1895) 301–19, 427–43; L. Laville, *Claude de Turin* (Montauban, 1889); M. Manitius 1 (Munich, 1911) 390–96; R. L. Poole, *Illustrations of the History of Mediaeval Thought* (London, 1920) pp. 24–33; Stegmüller 2, n. 1958.

5. Florus Diaconus [*ca.* 860]: *Carmina in Matthaeum et Iohannem: De gestis Domini.*
    Edit. E. Dümmler, MGH: *Poetae* 2 (1884) 509–23.

Lit. C. Charlier, "Les manuscrits personnels de Florus de Lyon et son activité littéraire," MEP (Lyons, 1945) pp. 71–84; Stegmüller 2, n. 2275.

6. Paschasius Radbertus [d. 860]: *Expositio in evangelium s. Matthaei.*
   Edit. PL 120, 31–994.
   Lit. H. Peltier; J. Hablitzel, SM 57 (1939) 113–16; A. E. Schönbach, SBW 146, 4 (Vienna, 1903) 142–74; Stegmüller 4, n. 6263.

7. Ps.-Alcuin [Irish: *ca.* 750–800]: *Liber quaestionum in evangeliis* (Commentarius in evangelium s. Matthaei).
   Edit. (partial) M. Manitius, "Ein Fragment aus einem Matthäuskommentar," ZKG 26 (1905) 235 ff.; F. Monier, *Alcuin et Charlemagne* (Paris, 1863) pp. 364 ff.; A. E. Schönbach, SBW 146, 4 (Vienna, 1903) 67–70.
   Lit. B. Bischoff, SE 6 (1954) 241–42; D. de Bruyne, "Une abbréviation inconnue," PLat 5 (1927) 48–49; D. de Bruyne, "Encore l'abbréviation de 'Haeret,' " PLat 6 (1929) 67–68; E. Dekkers, *Clavis patrum,* SE 3 (1951) n. 1168; Stegmüller 2, n. 1100.

8. Ps.-Bede [*ca.* 750–800]: *In Matthaei evangelium expositio.*
   Edit. PL 92, 9–132.
   Lit. F. J. E. Raby, "Bède le Vénérable," DHGE 7 (1934) 400; A. E. Schönbach, SBW 146, 4 (Vienna, 1903) 19–34; Stegmüller 2, n. 1678; 5, n. 7061.

9. Ps.-Jerome (Ps.-Walafrid Strabo) [Irish: *ca.* 650–700]: *Expositio quattuor evangeliorum: Expositio in Matthaeum.*
   Edit. PL 30, 531–60 (PL 114, 861–88). The manuscript tradition of this work presents three different recensions (Cf. B. Bischoff, SE 6 [1954] 236–37): Recension 1 (Ps.-Jerome), which is edited in Migne; Recension 2 (Ps.-Gregory) and Recension 3 (Traditio evangeliorum), which are unedited.
   Lit. B. Griesser, ZkTh 54 (1930) 40–87; B. Griesser, RBén 49 (1937) 279–321; E. Dekkers, *Clavis patrum,* SE 3 (1951) n. 631; Stegmüller 3, nn. 3424–27; 5, n. 8327.

10. Remigius of Auxerre [*ca.* 900]: *Homiliae duodecim.*
    Edit. PL 131, 865–932.
    Lit. A. E. Schönbach, SBW 146, 4 (Vienna, 1903) 174–75; J. Villar, "L'Expositio Remigii super Matthaeum en el cod. 548 de la Bibliotheca de Catalunya," *Estudis Univ. Catalana* 22 (1936) 263–81; Stegmüller 5, n. 7226.

11. Rhabanus Maurus [d. 856]: *Commentarius in s. Matthaeum.*
    Edit. (partial) E. Dümmler, MGH: *Epist.* 5 (1898) 388–90; F. Kunstmann, pp. 170–210.
    Lit. A. E. Schönbach, SBW 146, 4 (Vienna, 1903) 79–129; Stegmüller 5, n. 7060.

12. Sedulius Scottus [*ca.* 858]: *In argumentum evangelii Matthaei expositiuncula.*
    Edit. A. Mai, *Scriptorum veterum nova collectio* 9 (1837) 162–68; PL 103, 273–80.
    Lit. B. Bischoff, SE 6 (1954) 246–47; M. Esposito, PRIA 28 (1910) C, 64–65; J. Kenney 1, n. 373, ii; Stegmüller 5, n. 7603.

13. Walafrid Strabo [*ca.* 849]: *Homilia in initium evangelii secundum s. Matthaeum.*
    Edit. PL 114, 849–62; B. Pez, TAN 2 (Augsburg, 1721) 41–56.
    Lit. Stegmüller 5, n. 8326.

MARK

14. Bede [d. 735]: *Expositio evangelii secundum Marcum.*
    Edit. PL 92, 131–302.
    Lit. M. L. W. Laistner, JTS 34 (1933) 350–52; E. F. Sutcliffe, "Quotations in the Venerable Bede's Commentary on St. Mark," Bib 7 (1926) 428–39; Stegmüller 2, n. 1613.

15. Cummeanus (?) (Ps.-Jerome) [Irish: *ca.* 650]: *Expositio in Marcum.*
    Edit. PL 30, 609–68.
    Lit. B. Bischoff, SE 6 (1954) 200–202, 257–58.

16. Ps.-Jerome (Ps.-Walafrid Strabo) [Irish: *ca.* 650–700]: *Expositio quattuor evangeliorum: Expositio in Marcum.*
    Edit. PL 30, 560–67 (PL 114, 887–94).
    Lit. B. Griesser, ZkTh 54 (1930) 40–87; B. Griesser, RBén 49 (1937) 279–321; E. Dekkers, *Clavis patrum,* SE 3 (1951) n. 631; Stegmüller 3, n. 3425; 5, n. 8328.

17. Sedulius Scottus [*ca.* 858]: *In argumentum secundum Marcum expositiuncula.*
    Edit. A. Mai, *Scriptorum veterum nova collectio* 9 (1837) 170–75; PL 103, 279–86.
    Lit. M. Esposito, PRIA 28 (1910) C, 64–65; S. Hellmann, QULP 1 (Munich, 1906); M. L. W. Laistner, *Thought and Letters in Western Europe A.D. 500–900* (London, 1957) pp. 244, 319; Stegmüller 5, n. 7604.

LUKE

18. Bede [d. 735]: *In Lucae evangelium expositio.*
    Edit. PL 92, 301–634.
    Lit. M. L. W. Laistner, *Hand-list,* pp. 44–50; M. L. W. Laistner, JTS 34 (1933) 352–54; Stegmüller 2, n. 1614.

19. Christian of Stavelot (?): *Expositio brevis in Lucam evangelistam.*
    Edit. PL 106, 1503–14.
    Lit. M. L. W. Laistner, HTR 20 (1927) 129–32; J. Lebon, RHE 9 (1908) 453; C. Spicq, BT 26 (Paris, 1944) 49–50; Stegmüller 2, n. 1927.

[107]

20. Ps.-Jerome (Ps.-Walafrid Strabo) [Irish: *ca.* 650–700]: *Expositio quattuor evangeliorum: Expositio in Lucam.*
    Edit. PL 30, 567–77 (PL 114, 893–904).
    Lit. B. Griesser, ZkTh 54 (1930) 40–87; B. Griesser, RBén 49 (1937) 279–321; E. Dekkers, *Clavis patrum,* SE 3 (1951) n. 631; Stegmüller 3, n. 3426; 5, n. 8329.

21. Sedulius Scottus [*ca.* 858]: *In argumentum secundum Lucam expositiuncula.*
    Edit. PL 103, 285–90; A. Mai, *Scriptorum veterum nova collectio* 9 (1837) 177–81.
    Lit. M. Esposito, PRIA 28 (1910) C, 65; Stegmüller 5, n. 7605.

JOHN

22. Alcuin [d. 804]: *Commentaria in Ioannem.*
    Edit. PL 100, 737–1008; A. E. Schönbach, SBW 146, 4 (Vienna, 1903) 53 contains the prologue of the primitive version found in St. Gall 258.
    Lit. Stegmüller 2, n. 1096.

23. Christian of Stavelot (?): *Expositiuncula in Ioannem evangelistam.*
    Edit. PL 106, 1515–20.
    Lit. E. Dümmler, SBB (Berlin, 1890) pp. 935–52; M. L. W. Laistner, HTR 20 (1927) 129–32; J. Lebon, RHE 9 (1908) 453; A. E. Schönbach, SBW 146, 4 (Vienna, 1903) 174; C. Spicq, BT 26 (Paris, 1944) 49–50; Stegmüller 2, n. 1928.

24. Florus Diaconus [d. 860]: *Carmina in Matthaeum et Iohannem: De gestis Christi.*
    Edit. E. Dümmler, MGH: *Poetae* 2 (1884) 509–23.
    Lit. Stegmüller 2, n. 2275.

25. John Scotus Eriugena [*ca.* 867]: *Commentarius in sanctum evangelium secundum Iohannem.*
    Edit. PL 122, 297–348, 1243–50; F. Ravaisson, *Catalogue général* 1 (Laon, 1849) 504–68; M. Saint-René Taillandier, *Scot Erigène* (Strassburg, 1843) p. 299.
    Lit. H. Bett, *Johannes Scotus Erigena* (Cambridge, 1925); M. Cappuyns, *Jean Scot Erigène, sa vie, son oeuvre, sa pensée* (Louvain, 1933); J. Kenney 1, n. 395; M. Manitius 1 (Munich, 1911) 323–39; 2 (Munich, 1923) 803; Stegmüller 3, n. 4959.

26. John Scotus Eriugena [*ca.* 867]: *Homilia in prologum evangelii secundum Iohannem.*
    Edit. PL 122, 283–96.
    Lit. Cf. n. 25 supra.

27. Ps.-Bede (Alcuin ?): *In s. Ioannis evangelium expositio.*
    Edit. PL 92, 633–938.

Lit. A. E. Schönbach, SBW 146, 4 (Vienna, 1903) 34–42; Stegmüller 2, n. 1680.

28. Ps.-Jerome (Ps.-Walafrid Strabo) [Irish: *ca.* 650–700]: *Expositio quattuor evangeliorum: Expositio in Iohannem.*

Edit. PL 30, 577–90 (PL 114, 903–16).

Lit. B. Griesser, ZkTh 54 (1930) 40–87; B. Griesser, RBén 49 (1937) 279–321; E. Dekkers, *Clavis patrum,* SE 3 (1951) n. 631; Stegmüller 3, n. 3427; 5, n. 8330.

ACTS

29. Bede [d. 735]: *Expositio Actuum Apostolorum.*

Edit. M. L. W. Laistner (Cambridge, Mass., 1939) pp. 1–90; PL 92, 937–96.

Lit. M. L. W. Laistner, "The Latin Version of the Acts Known to the Venerable Bede," HTR 30 (1937) 37–50; Stegmüller 2, n. 1615.

30. Bede [d. 735]: *Retractatio in Actibus Apostolorum.*

Edit. M. L. W. Laistner (Cambridge, Mass., 1939) pp. 91–146; PL 92, 995–1032.

Lit. Stegmüller 2, n. 1616.

31. Bede [d. 735]: *De nominibus locorum vel civitatum quae leguntur in loco Actuum Apostolorum.*

Edit. M. L. W. Laistner (Cambridge, Mass., 1939) pp. 147–58; PL 92, 1033–40.

Lit. Stegmüller 2, n. 1618.

32. Ps.-Bede: *Expositio Actuum Apostolorum.*

Edit. PL 92, 1031–34.

Lit. Stegmüller 2, n. 1682.

ROMANS

33. Claude of Turin [*ca.* 840]: *Commentarius in epistulam ad Romanos* (Eulogium s. Augustini).

Edit. (partial) PL 104, 927–28; Preface, ed. E. Dümmler, MGH: *Epist.* 4 (1895) 599–600; H. Denifle 1 (Mainz, 1905) nn. 12–13; W. Affeldt, *Die Auslegung von Röm. 13, 1–7 von Origenes bis zum Ende des 13 Jahr.* (Berlin, 1956) pp. 368–73.

Lit. W. Affeldt, Trad 13 (1957) 378; Stegmüller 2, n. 1959.

34. Florus Diaconus [*ca.* 860]: *Expositio in epistulam ad Romanos.*

Edit. PL 119, 279–318.

Lit. W. Affeldt, Trad 13 (1957) 379; C. Charlier, "Les manuscrits personnels de Florus et son activité littéraire," MEP (Lyons, 1945) pp. 71–84; C. Charlier, "La compilation augustinienne de Florus sur l'Apôtre," RBén 57 (1947) 132–86; A. Wilmart, "La collection de Bède le Vénérable sur l'Apôtre," RBén 38 (1926) 16–52; A. Wilmart, "Sommaire de l'Exposition de Florus sur les Epîtres," RBén 38 (1926) 205–14; A.

[109]

Wilmart, "Notes sur Florus et Mannon," RBén 38 (1926) 214–16; A. Wilmart, "Le mythe de Pierre de Tripoli," RBén 43 (1931) 347–52; Stegmüller 2, n. 2277; 4, n. 6920.

35. Hatto of Vercelli [d. 961]: *Expositio in epistulam ad Romanos.*
   Edit. PL 134, 125–288.
   Lit. W. Affeldt, Trad 13 (1957) 383; S. Hellmann, QULP 1 (Munich, 1906) 182, n. 7; M. Manitius 2 (Munich, 1923) 28–29, 32; E. Riggenbach, pp. 25–30; A. Souter, TSt 9 (Cambridge, 1922) 322, n. 3; C. Spicq, BT 26 (Paris, 1944) 54; Stegmüller 3, n. 3126.

36. Haymo of Auxerre (Ps.-Haymo of Halberstadt) [*ca.* 865] *Expositio in epistulam ad Romanos.*
   Edit. PL 117, 361–508.
   Lit. W. Affeldt, Trad 13 (1957) 382–83; H. Denifle 1 (Mainz, 1905) nn. 18–22; H. H. Glunz, p. 102; M. Manitius 1 (Munich, 1911) 516–17; E. Riggenbach, pp. 41–201; B. Smalley, *The Study of the Bible in the Middle Ages* (Oxford, 1952) pp. 39–40; A. Souter, TSt 9 (Cambridge, 1922) 339–41; C. Spicq, BT 26 (Paris, 1944) 50–51; Stegmüller 3, nn. 3071, 3101–14.

37. Rhabanus Maurus [d. 856]: *Enarratio in epistulam ad Romanos.*
   Edit. PL 111, 1273–1616; Preface, ed. E. Dümmler, MGH: *Epist.* 5 (1898) 429–30.
   Lit. W. Affeldt, Trad 13 (1957) 399–400; E. Dümmler, SBB (Berlin, 1898) pp. 34–42; H. H. Glunz, p. 97; J. B. Hablitzel, BS 11 (1906); J. B. Hablitzel, "Hrabanus Maurus und Claudius von Turin," HJ 27 (1906) 74–85; 38 (1917) 538–52; M. Manitius 1 (Munich, 1911) 290–91; E. Riggenbach, pp. 33–37; A. E. Schönbach, SBW 146, 4 (Vienna, 1903) 91; C. Spicq, BT 26 (Paris, 1944) 16–21, 22–24, 38–44; Stegmüller 5, n. 7064.

38. Sedulius Scottus [*ca.* 858]: *Collectanea in epistulam ad Romanos.*
   Edit. PL 103, 9–128.
   Lit. W. Affeldt, Trad 13 (1957) 401–402; S. Hellmann, QULP 1 (Munich, 1906) 147; E. Riggenbach, pp. 212–27; A. Souter, "The Sources of Sedulius Scottus's Collectaneum on the Epistles of St. Paul," JTS 18 (1917) 184–228; A. Souter, TSt 9 (Cambridge, 1922) 336; C. Spicq, BT 26 (Paris, 1944) 45; Stegmüller 5, n. 7608.

39. Tietlandus (?) [d. 964]: *Commentarius in epistulam ad Romanos.*
   Edit. (partial) H. Denifle, nn. 27–28.
   Lit. W. Affeldt, Trad 13 (1957) 404; Stegmüller 5, n. 8267.

CORINTHIANS 1–2

40. Claude of Turin [*ca.* 840]: *Praefatio.*
   Edit. Preface, ed. E. Dümmler, MGH: *Epist.* 4 (1895) 600–602; PL 104, 837–40.
   Lit. Stegmüller 2, nn. 1960–61.

41. Florus Diaconus [d. 860]: *Expositio in epistulas ad Corinthios.*
     Edit. PL 119, 317–64.
     Lit. Stegmüller 2, nn. 2278–79; 4, nn. 6921–22.

42. Hatto of Vercelli [d. 961]: *Expositio in epistulas ad Corinthios.*
     Edit. PL 134, 287–492.
     Lit. M. Manitius 2 (Munich, 1923) 27–34; A. Souter, TSt 9 (Cambridge, 1922) 332–33; Stegmüller 3, nn. 3127–28.

43. Haymo of Auxerre (Ps.-Haymo of Halberstadt) [*ca.* 865]: *Expositio in epistulas ad Corinthios.*
     Edit. PL 117, 507–668.
     Lit. Stegmüller 3, nn. 3071, 3101–14.

44. Rhabanus Maurus [d. 856]: *Expositio in epistulas ad Corinthios.*
     Edit. PL 112, 9–246.
     Lit. Stegmüller 5, nn. 7065–66.

45. Sedulius Scottus [*ca.* 858]: *Collectanea in epistulas ad Corinthios.*
     Edit. PL 103, 127–82.
     Lit. Stegmüller 5, nn. 7609–10.

GALATIANS

46. Claude of Turin [*ca.* 840]: *Enarratio in epistulam ad Galatas.*
     Edit. PL 104, 841–912.
     Lit. Stegmüller 2, n. 1962.

47. Florus Diaconus [d. 860]: *Expositio in epistulam ad Galatas.*
     Edit. PL 119, 363–74.
     Lit. Stegmüller 2, n. 2280; 4, n. 6923.

48. Hatto of Vercelli [d. 961]: *Expositio in epistulam ad Galatas.*
     Edit. PL 134, 491–546.
     Lit. Stegmüller 3, n. 3129.

49. Haymo of Auxerre (Ps.-Haymo of Halberstadt) [*ca.* 865]: *Expositio in epistulam ad Galatas.*
     Edit. PL 117, 669–700.
     Lit. Stegmüller 3, nn. 3071, 3104.

50. Rhabanus Maurus [d. 856]: *Expositio in epistulam ad Galatas.*
     Edit. PL 112, 245–382.
     Lit. Stegmüller 5, n. 7067.

51. Sedulius Scottus [*ca.* 858]: *Collectaneum in epistulam ad Galatas.*
     Edit. PL 103, 181–94.
     Lit. Stegmüller 5, n. 7611.

EPHESIANS

52. Claude of Turin [*ca.* 840]: *Commentarius in epistulam ad Ephesios.*
     Edit. Preface, ed. E. Dümmler, MGH: *Epist.* 4 (1895) 597–99; PL 104, 839–42.
     Lit. Stegmüller 2, n. 1963.

[111]

53. Florus Diaconus [d. 860]: *Expositio in epistulam ad Ephesios.*
    Edit. PL 119, 373–82.
    Lit. Stegmüller 2, n. 2281; 4, n. 6924.

54. Hatto of Vercelli [d. 961]: *Expositio in epistulam ad Ephesios.*
    Edit. PL 134, 545–86.
    Lit. Stegmüller 3, n. 3130.

55. Haymo of Auxerre (Ps.-Haymo of Halberstadt) [*ca.* 865]: *Expositio in epistulam ad Ephesios.*
    Edit. PL 117, 699–734.
    Lit. Stegmüller 3, nn. 3071, 3105.

56. Rhabanus Maurus [d. 856]: *Expositio in epistulam ad Ephesios.*
    Edit. PL 112, 381–478.
    Lit. Stegmüller 5, n. 7068.

57. Sedulius Scottus [*ca.* 858]: *Collectaneum in epistulam ad Ephesios.*
    Edit. PL 103, 195–212.
    Lit. Stegmüller 5, n. 7612.

PHILIPPIANS

58. Florus Diaconus [d. 860]: *Expositio in epistulam ad Philippenses.*
    Edit. PL 119, 381–90.
    Lit. Stegmüller 2, n. 2282; 4, n. 6925.

59. Hatto of Vercelli [d. 961]: *Expositio in epistulam ad Philippenses.*
    Edit. PL 134, 585–608.
    Lit. Stegmüller 3, n. 3131.

60. Haymo of Auxerre (Ps.-Haymo of Halberstadt) [*ca.* 865]: *Expositio in epistulam ad Philippenses.*
    Edit. PL 117, 735–54.
    Lit. Stegmüller 3, nn. 3071, 3106, 3101–14.

61. Rhabanus Maurus [d. 856]: *Enarratio in epistulam ad Philippenses.*
    Edit. PL 112, 477–508.
    Lit. Stegmüller 5, n. 7069.

62. Sedulius Scottus [*ca.* 858]: *Collectaneum in epistulam ad Philippenses.*
    Edit. PL 105, 211–18.
    Lit. Stegmüller 5, n. 7613.

COLOSSIANS

63. Florus Diaconus [d. 860]: *Expositio in epistulam ad Colossenses.*
    Edit. PL 119, 389–94.
    Lit. Stegmüller 2, n. 2283; 4, n. 6926.

64. Hatto of Vercelli [d. 961]: *Expositio in epistulam ad Colossenses.*
    Edit. PL 134, 609–44.
    Lit. Stegmüller 3, n. 3132.

[112]

65. Haymo of Auxerre (Ps.-Haymo of Halberstadt) [ca. 865]: *Expositio in epistulam ad Colossenses.*
    Edit. PL 117, 753–66.
    Lit. Stegmüller 3, nn. 3071, 3109, 3101–14.

66. Rhabanus Maurus [d. 856]: *Expositio in epistulam ad Colossenses.*
    Edit. PL 112, 507–40.
    Lit. Stegmüller 5, n. 7070.

67. Sedulius Scottus [ca. 858]: *Collectaneum in epistulam ad Colossenses.*
    Edit. PL 103, 223–30.
    Lit. Stegmüller 5, nn. 7614, 7607–21.

THESSALONIANS 1–2

68. Florus Diaconus [d. 860]: *Expositio in epistulas ad Thessalonicenses.*
    Edit. PL 119, 393–98.
    Lit. Stegmüller 2, nn. 2284–85; 4, nn. 6927–28.

69. Hatto of Vercelli [d. 961]: *Expositio in epistulas ad Thessalonicenses.*
    Edit. PL 134, 643–64.
    Lit. Stegmüller 3, nn. 3133–34; 2, nn. 1256–57.

70. Haymo of Auxerre (Ps.-Haymo of Halberstadt) [ca. 865]: *Expositio in epistulas ad Thessalonicenses.*
    Edit. PL 117, 765–84.
    Lit. Stegmüller 3, nn. 3071, 3107–3108, 3101–3104.

71. Rhabanus Maurus [d. 856]: *Enarratio in epistulas ad Thessalonicenses.*
    Edit. PL 112, 539–80.
    Lit. Stegmüller 5, nn. 7071–72.

72. Sedulius Scottus [ca. 858]: *Collectanea in epistulas ad Thessalonicenses.*
    Edit. PL 103, 217–24.
    Lit. Stegmüller 5, nn. 7615–16, 7607–21.

TIMOTHY 1–2

73. Florus Diaconus [d. 860]: *Expositio in epistulas ad Timotheum.*
    Edit. PL 119, 397–410.
    Lit. Stegmüller 2, nn. 2286–87; 4, nn. 6929–30.

74. Hatto of Vercelli [d. 961]: *Expositio in epistulas ad Timotheum.*
    Edit. PL 134, 663–700.
    Lit. Stegmüller 3, nn. 3135–36; 2, nn. 1258–59.

75. Haymo of Auxerre (Ps.-Haymo of Halberstadt) [ca. 865]: *Expositio in epistulas ad Timotheum.*
    Edit. PL 117, 783–810.
    Lit. Stegmüller 3, nn. 3071, 3110–11, 3101–14.

76. Rhabanus Maurus [d. 856]: *Enarratio in epistulas ad Timotheum.*
    Edit. PL 112, 579–654.
    Lit. Stegmüller 5, nn. 7073–74.

[113]

77. Sedulius Scottus [*ca.* 858]: *Collectanea in epistulas ad Timotheum.*
    Edit. PL 103, 229–42.
    Lit. Stegmüller 5, nn. 7617–18, 7607–21.

TITUS

78. Alcuin [d. 804]: *Tractatus super epistulam ad Titum.*
    Edit. PL 100, 1009–26.
    Lit. Stegmüller 2, n. 1097.

79. Florus Diaconus [d. 860]: *Expositio in epistulam ad Titum.*
    Edit. PL 119, 409–10.
    Lit. Stegmüller 2, n. 2288; 4, n. 6931.

80. Hatto of Vercelli [d. 961]: *Expositio in epistulam ad Titum.*
    Edit. PL 134, 699–720.
    Lit. Stegmüller 3, n. 3137.

81. Haymo of Auxerre (Ps.-Haymo of Halberstadt) [*ca.* 865]: *Expositio in epistulam ad Titum.*
    Edit. PL 117, 809–14.
    Lit. Stegmüller 3, nn. 3071, 3112, 3101–14.

82. Rhabanus Maurus [d. 856]: *Enarratio in epistulam ad Titum.*
    Edit. PL 112, 653–92.
    Lit. Stegmüller 5, n. 7075.

83. Sedulius Scottus [*ca.* 858]: *Collectaneum in epistulam ad Titum.*
    Edit. PL 103, 241–50.
    Lit. Stegmüller 5, nn. 7619, 7607–21.

PHILEMON

84. Alcuin [d. 804]: *Tractatus super epistulam ad Philemonem.*
    Edit. PL 100, 1025–32.
    Lit. Stegmüller 2, n. 1098.

85. Claude of Turin [*ca.* 840]: *Expositio epistulae ad Philemonem.*
    Edit. PL 104, 911–18.
    Lit. Stegmüller 2, n. 1971.

86. Claude of Turin (?): *Expositio epistulae ad Philemonem.*
    Edit. A. Mai, *Spicilegium Romanum* 9, 109–17.
    Lit. Stegmüller 2, n. 1972.

87. Florus Diaconus [d. 860]: *Expositio in epistulam ad Philemonem.*
    Edit. PL 119, 411–12.
    Lit. Stegmüller 2, n. 2289; 4, n. 6932.

88. Hatto of Vercelli [d. 961]: *Expositio in epistulam ad Philemonem.*
    Edit. PL 134, 719–26.
    Lit. Stegmüller 3, n. 3138.

89. Haymo of Auxerre (Ps.-Haymo of Halberstadt) [*ca.* 865]: *Expositio in epistulam ad Philemonem.*

[114]

Edit. PL 117, 813–20.
Lit. Stegmüller 3, nn. 3071, 3113, 3101–14.

90. Rhabanus Maurus [d. 856]: Enarratio in epistulam ad Philemonem.
Edit. PL 112, 693–712.
Lit. Stegmüller 5, n. 7076.

91. Sedulius Scottus [ca. 858]: Collectaneum in epistulam ad Philemonem.
Edit. PL 103, 249–52.
Lit. Stegmüller 5, n. 7620.

HEBREWS

92. Alcuin (?): Tractatus super epistulam ad Hebraeos.
Edit. PL 100, 1031–84.
Lit. Stegmüller 2, n. 1099.

93. Anonymous (Ps.-Pelagius) [Irish: 650–800]: Expositio epistulae Pauli apostoli ad Hebraeos.
Edit. H. Zimmer, Pelagius in Irland (Berlin, 1901) pp. 420–48.
Lit. W. Affeldt, Trad 13 (1957) 393; B. Bischoff, SE 6 (1954) 268.

94. Claude of Turin [ca. 840]: Expositio in epistulam ad Hebraeos.
Edit. PL 134, 725–834.
Lit. Stegmüller 2, nn. 1973–74; 3, n. 3139.

95. Florus Diaconus [d. 860]: Expositio in epistulam ad Hebraeos.
Edit. PL 119, 411–20.
Lit. Stegmüller 2, n. 2290; 4, n. 6933.

96. Haymo of Auxerre (Ps.-Haymo of Halberstadt) [ca. 865]: Expositio in epistulam ad Hebraeos.
Edit. PL 117, 819–938.
Lit. Stegmüller 3, nn. 3114, 3071.

97. Ps.-Jerome: Expositio in epistulam ad Hebraeos.
Edit. (partial) E. Riggenbach, pp. 206–12.
Lit. B. Bischoff, SE 6 (1954) 269; E. Riggenbach, p. 205; Stegmüller 3, n. 3455.

98. Rhabanus Maurus [d. 856]: Enarratio in epistulam ad Hebraeos.
Edit. PL 112, 711–834.
Lit. Stegmüller 5, n. 7077.

99. Sedulius Scottus [ca. 858]: Collectaneum in epistulam ad Hebraeos.
Edit. PL 103, 251–70.
Lit. Stegmüller 5, n. 7621.

JAMES

100. Bede [d. 735]: Expositio in epistulam Iacobi.
Edit. PL 93, 9–42.
Lit. E. Dekkers, Clavis patrum, SE 3 (1951) n. 1362; Stegmüller 2, n. 1632.

[115]

PETER 1–2

101. Bede [d. 735]: *Expositio in epistulas Petri.*
   Edit. PL 93, 41–86.
   Lit. E. Dekkers, *Clavis patrum,* SE 3 (1951) n. 1362; Stegmüller 2, nn. 1633–34.

JOHN 1–3

102. Bede [d. 735]: *Expositio in epistulas Ioannis.*
   Edit. PL 93, 85–124.
   Lit. E. Dekkers, *Clavis patrum,* SE 3 (1951) n. 1362; Stegmüller 2, nn. 1635–37.

JUDE

103. Bede [d. 735]: *Expositio in epistulam Iudae.*
   Edit. PL 93, 123–30.
   Lit. E. Dekkers, *Clavis patrum,* SE 3 (1951) n. 1638; Stegmüller 2, n. 1638.

APOCALYPSE

104. Alcuin (?) (Ps.-Bede): *Commentarius in Apocalypsin.*
   Edit. PL 100, 1087–1156.
   Lit. A. Wilmart, *Auteurs spirituels et textes dévots du moyen âge latin* (Paris, 1932) p. 52, n. 6; Stegmüller 2, nn. 1102, 1684.

105. Ambrosius Autpertus [*ca.* 781]: *Commentarius in Apocalypsin.*
   Edit. MBP 13 (Lyons, 1677) 403–657.
   Lit. H. Riedlinger, "Ambrosius Autpertus," *Lexikon für Theologie und Kirche* 1 (1957) 426; Stegmüller 2, n. 1275.

106. Beatus of Liébana [d. 798]: *Commentarius in Apocalypsin.*
   Edit. H. A. Sanders, *Beati in Apocalipsin libri duodecim,* in *Papers and Monographs of the American Academy in Rome* 7 (Rome, 1930); A. Vega, *España sagrada* 56 (Madrid, 1957).
   Lit. M. del Alamo, "Los comentarios de Beato al Apocalipsis y Elipando," ST 122 (Rome, 1946) 16–33; W. Kamlah, HS 285 (Berlin, 1935); W. Neuss, *Die Apokalypse des hl. Johannes in der altspanischen und altchristlichen Bibelillustration* (Münster, 1931); T. Rojo Orcajo, *Estudios de códices visigóticos. El "Beato" de la biblioteca de Santa Cruz de Valladolid* (Madrid, 1930); F. C. Sainz de Robles, *Elipando y san Beato de Liébana, siglo VIII* (Madrid, 1935); H. Vogels, *Untersuchungen zur Geschichte der lateinischen Apokalypse-Übersetzung* (Düsseldorf, 1920); W. H. Whitehall, "A Beatus-fragment at Santo Domingo de Silos," Spec 4 (1929) 102–5; Stegmüller 2, n. 1597.

107. Bede [d. 735]: *Explanatio Apocalypsis.*
   Edit. PL 93, 129–206.

[116]

Lit. E. Dekkers, *Clavis patrum,* SE 3 (1951) n. 1363; Stegmüller 2, n. 1640. *

108. Berengaudus [*ca.* 859]: *Expositio super septem visiones libri Apocalypsis.*
   Edit. PL 17, 843–1058.
   Lit. A. Harnack, *Geschichte der altchristlichen Literatur* 1 (Leipzig, 1893) 264; W. Kamlah, HS 285 (Berlin, 1935) 15; Stegmüller 2, n. 1711.

109. Haymo of Auxerre (Ps.-Haymo of Halberstadt) [*ca.* 865]: *Expositio in Apocalypsin b. Ioannis.*
   Edit. PL 117, 937–1220.
   Lit. E. Riggenbach; L. Traube, MGH: *Poetae* 3 (1896) 422; Stegmüller 3, nn. 3072, 3122; 5, n. 7247.

110. Ps.-Isidore (Ps.-Augustine, Ps.-Jerome) [Irish: *ca.* 800]: *Commentarius de Apocalipsi.*
   Edit. K. Hartung, *Ein Traktat zur Apokalypse des Apostels Johannes* (Bamberg, 1904).
   Lit. B. Bischoff, SE 6 (1954) 272; E. Dekkers, *Clavis patrum,* SE 3 (1951) n. 1221; J. Haussleiter, *Victorini episcopi Petavionensis opera,* CSEL 49 (Vienna, 1916) xlvii f.; Stegmüller 3, n. 5271.

[117]

★ Index ★

[119]